A Dating Memoir

Did He Really Just Do That?

150 Dates With 75 Guys In 1 Year
My Mission to Find Love

Valerie Margo

DEDICATION

This book is dedicated to all the guys I dated. To the guys who found their way into this memoir and played a role in my personal journey, this is my interpretation of our interactions, and I acknowledge that your version of the events may differ from mine. Regardless, I am grateful for the moments we shared and the ways in which you helped me grow. Thank you for the experiences, for being a part of my story, and for inspiring me to share it with others. I would not have evolved to where I am without you.

Disclaimer

This memoir is a personal account of the author's experiences. Nicknames were given for discretion, to safeguard identities. The author aims for accuracy, but artistic choices could affect the details. Remember, this memoir is for entertainment and to provoke personal reflection. Understand that this is the author's unique story. The author isn't responsible for how you interpret it.

CONTENTS

Acknowledgments   i

1   My Motto & My Mission   1

2   Getting Started   4

3   The Rebounds   24

4   Is Chemistry Important?   45

5   Could He Be My Person?   79

6   No Emotional Attachment   108

7   Am I Ready to be in a Relationship?   144

8   What's Up with the Nice Guys?   165

9   No Expectations   193

10   Epilogue   241

ACKNOWLEDGMENTS

Thank you to The Writer With 2 N's for inspiring me to write this memoir. To Jianny Adamo who encouraged me to take a memoir writing class, Barbara Cronie who taught it, and the critiquing group, I'd like to express my gratitude.

I'd like to extend a special thank you to my best friend D, who was there for me throughout, did a last reading with me out loud, and her viewpoints. Also, to Jenn for proofreading, to Karen for listening, and Melissa for giving great advice.

I'd like to acknowledge Don (he calls me his Pickleball wife) for spending a great amount of time with me editing this memoir, along with his positive feedback.

To my daughter for additional editing, my son for designing the front and back cover, and to M for giving me your invaluable perspective and unwavering support, I am forever grateful.

To my therapist who educated me, motivated me, and counseled me throughout my process, I'm thankful.

To my colorist Alex for taking the pic for the back cover in just the right pose, much appreciated.

Thank you to everyone who has helped me in this journey of writing and publishing my memoir. Your support and encouragement mean the world to me.

1
MY MOTTO & MY MISSION

My Motto: Timing, Luck, and Perseverance. These three words are guiding principles and serve as my personal motto.

I believe that timing and good luck are usually channeled by the power of fate, but it's perseverance that sets us apart to help achieve our goals. We can't just set an intention, it's not enough. Perseverance is the steadfast determination to never give up, even in the face of obstacles and setbacks. Perseverance absolutely makes the difference.

Whether it's pursuing our dreams or navigating relationships, we must put forth effort and persevere through the ups and downs. Love isn't something that just happens. We can't wait around for our person to show up and sweep us off our feet. Instead, we must put ourselves out there, take risks, and persevere through challenges.

My Mission: I'm always on a mission. My mission in this instance was to find inner peace, happiness, and love in my life.

I was newly separated from my husband. My life was in turmoil, and I needed diversion. Diversion from all the shit going on. Although it seemed premature, I decided to get back out there and start online dating. It had been 25 years since I'd been on a date.

From my first chapter, "Getting Started," to the second, "Rebounds," then "Is Chemistry Important?" I continued my quest to find love and went on over 150 dates with more than 75 guys in one year.

The format of this self-help memoir remains the same throughout. I gave each guy a nickname, and subsequently exposed his character traits and/or specific behaviors. I recounted each story in my own voice, my version of the events. Red flags, then insights and lessons learned are revealed and listed. It's important to note, some of the stories overlapped on my timeline before the next chapter begins.

You will see how I evolved that year from being vulnerable to feeling more confident, gaining my self-esteem back, and ultimately, feeling empowered. Finally understanding my worth and what I deserved, I remained determined to find someone to share my life with.

I encourage you to take your own journey of self-discovery and growth. Date with a good attitude. Have fun. Open your heart. Read my stories. Gain some insight. Use the red flags, insights and lessons learned as a tool to learn from my mistakes before you make them yourself. Be cognizant. Use your intuition. Set your boundaries. This is what I did, and hopefully this inspires and empowers you too.

2

GETTING STARTED

November

Kayak Guy: *The Self-Proclaimed Online Dating Pro*

What did I know about online dating? A big fat nothing! I was 50 years old, had just separated from my husband, and hadn't been on a date in 25 years.

"How long have you been separated?" Kayak Guy asked me.

"Two months."

"That's it?"

"Yup. I just got online this week."

"No wonder why I haven't seen you online before. Don't you think it's a bit soon for you to be dating, especially online?"

"I thought I would give it a try. I have a girlfriend who's been online for years. She says it's easy. She's looking for her fourth husband, LOL."

"Well then, you will need some pointers. It's not easy."

"Really?"

"I've been on these sites for a while. You have no idea what you are about to encounter."

"How long have you been online?"

"Years."

He started giving me the lowdown on online dating. After all his warnings he seemed tentative but set up a lunch date with me anyway.

I was keyed up as I drove to meet him for lunch. *I hope he looks as good as his pics. I hope he is as nice as he appears to be.* The "I hope" rambled on in my head.

I waited outside the restaurant for him to arrive. Minutes passed. I stood there impatiently. Finally! He smiled as he got closer. I smiled back. A bit of relief came over me. He had a cute look, cute dimples in his cheeks, light brown hair, not too tall, and was lean.

"Hi." He smiled.

"Hi. What happened there? Are you okay?" I was looking at the dried-up blood on his cheek.

"Yeah, I'm okay. I cut myself shaving which I never do. I guess I'm nervous."

"You . . . nervous? I thought you were the online dating pro?"

He didn't answer. He opened the door and we walked into the restaurant.

"I'm surprised you picked this place to meet. It's not the type of place I thought you'd choose."

"Well, it was the only place I could find in this area that was open for lunch."

"I got a feeling you would have liked the trendy place I would have chosen in West Palm."

"I'm sure I would've, but that was too far for me to drive."

I was impressed he already had a read on me.

"You said you're newly separated. What's your situation?" Kayak Guy asked me.

"I was married for 24 years. I'm getting divorced. I have two kids, 15 and 20. My son is in college and my daughter in high school."

"That's a long time."

"Yup. Too long."

"I've been divorced for over 18 years and have two grown up daughters."

"You've been divorced for a long time. Have you been in any relationships since?"

"I've had a few short ones."

"After all this online dating you haven't found anyone?"

"No, unfortunately not."

"Why do you think that is?" I asked.

"I'm not sure. I told you it's crazy out there. There are a lot of people with a lot of baggage."

"Oh. Thanks for reminding me."

"Yes. Keep your eyes open."

He got more specific and started giving me additional advice.

"Have you ever gone kayaking?" He asked.

"No."

"I spend lots of time with my bros and we go kayaking a lot."

"Nice. You're an Aerospace Engineer, right?"

"Yes."

"Can you tell me about your career, it seems interesting?"

He talked about all his kayaking adventures with his bros. He had little to say about himself or about his career. I was getting bored. I told him more specific things about my life. I talked too much to keep the conversation flowing.

"I have to go now." I said to him.

As we walked to my car, I gave him a flirty smile. He was easy on the eyes. He took ahold of my arm with a gentle touch.

"It was nice meeting you. Thanks for the advice." I smiled.

He leaned in and kissed me. *Hello.* He kissed me deeper. *Arousing!* I came up for air and looked around.

"Luckily this parking lot is fairly empty." I jested.

"Who cares." He shrugged his shoulders.

We started kissing again. He was a pretty good kisser. It felt good. I didn't remember what decent kissing was like, since before my marriage 25 years ago.

"I'd better get going." I said, looking at my watch.

I waved as I drove away with a smile on my face.

Our make out session was totally unexpected. He'd given me no clue he was even the least bit interested in me, other than taking me under his wing and giving me online dating advice.

A few days later Kayak Guy called. He had nothing interesting to say. I was bored again. I thought he would ask me out. Why did he call?

He called again a few days later on Thanksgiving. He droned on about the food he was cooking. Again, I was waiting for him to ask me out, but he never did.

Red Flags
- ❖ I was bored.
- ❖ He wasn't interesting.
- ❖ He hadn't been in a relationship in years.

Insights and Lessons Learned
- ❖ He gave good advice, but he was no dating pro.

November

Mr. Boner: *The Pushy, Vile, Drunken, Misogynist*

"Meet me down at Sawgrass Mills. It's close to my accounting firm and home." Mr. Boner said.

"I'm sorry, Sawgrass is too far for me."

"I'm working until 7:30, so it would be easier for me if you drove down this way. Come on . . . just come down here."

Why is he being so pushy?

"I'm sorry. I'm only willing to drive 15 minutes. Otherwise, we will have to make it another time."

"Well, okay. Meet me at Bonefish Grill in Coral Springs. I'll see you at the bar at 8:00."

It was my second date of the day. Would my date with Mr. Boner be more stimulating than Kayak Guy? I certainly hope so.

I drove in a nervous frenzy, then walked into the bar and saw Mr. Boner laughing with some guy standing next to him. He was much lankier than I expected. He towered over me. He turned towards me, held his glass up high, and took a sip of his martini.

"Hi." I greeted him.

He smiled at me and took his last gulp.

"Bartender, I'll have two more Lemon Drop Martinis. I'm getting one for you."

"No thanks."

"Oh, come on. It's just a Lemon Drop."

Mr. Boner turned to grab the martinis. As he turned around, he jostled the glasses. I flinched and leaned back to avoid a spill. He put the glass to my lips. I took a sip.

"That's good, isn't it?"

"Yes." I took the glass from him.

We got acquainted. Then, Mr. Boner went to the hostess stand, and came back.

"The table's ready."

Mr. Boner took my martini and motioned to follow the hostess. We passed a group of women who were laughing and having fun.

"You look so sexy. I bet those women are jealous of you." He whispered in my ear.

That comment seemed bizarre. He put the martini down in front of me.

"Don't waste your Lemon Drop."

I took a sip to appease him. He was guzzling his.

"Do you like mussels?" Mr. Boner was gazing at the menu.

"Yes."

"Hi. Are you ready to order?" The waiter greeted us.

"I'll have another Lemon Drop, and we'll have the mussels and parmesan-crusted trout dish."

"Wow, those Lemon Drops are going down easy." I said, in a flippant tone.

"I had a hard day at work. Don't let that drink just sit there. Drink up."

Mr. Boner's third martini arrived.

"These are tasty, aren't they?" He held up his glass.

"Yes, they are."

The waiter arrived and placed the mussels on the table. I took my spoon and stuck it in the bowl. He put his hand on mine to stop me. Mr. Boner then put his fingers into the bowl, took hold of a mussel, and with his fork, pulled it from the shell. He then put it to my mouth. I hesitated but ate it. I didn't know what else to do.

"I can feed myself, thank you." I said to him.

He put his fingers in the bowl again, pulled out another mussel, and ate it. I started to cringe. No more mussels for me.

"My ex is so stupid! I gave her millions and all she did when we were married was sit on her ass with the maid watching Telenovelas, and she didn't even understand Español."

He shook his head while eating, then continued ranting about her. I felt perturbed. Mr. Boner was sloshed. I asked him to refrain from talking about his ex-wife. He kept on anyway.

"One night I was with my ex-girlfriend. We were going at it so hard . . . the sheets were so bloody."

He was laughing while he finished his third martini. *I have to get out of here. He's a disgusting pig!*

"Can you please stop the vile talk. I need to get home now."

He didn't listen. I sat there cowering. I excused myself and went to the restroom. I took some deep breaths and went back to the table.

"I need to leave now." I said again.

Finally, he paid the check. I got up and quickly left the restaurant. I could feel his presence behind me. *Walk faster!* As I reached for the car door, I felt his hand on my left shoulder. He spun me around to face him. Mr. Boner pressed my back onto my car, put his hands on both sides of me, and fenced me in. He looked at me as if I was a bullseye on a dartboard. He bent his arms in like he was doing a push-up. He started slobbering all over me. He tried jamming his tongue in my mouth. I smelled and tasted the mussels mixed with the Lemon Drop. Nauseating! Then, I felt his spindly boner as he pressed his gangly, drunken body against me. *WTF!* I pushed him away.

"Get away! Go home."

He smirked, then moseyed away like he had just caught the biggest fish of the day. I got in my car and got out of there.

Did he really just do that? Maybe I should heed Kayak Guy's warning?

Mr. Boner messaged me the next day and asked me out. I messaged him back and told him his behavior was inexcusable. He apologized, then proceeded to ask me out again. I expressed to him that I wasn't interested, and not to contact me again.

Weeks later, he messaged me again. I didn't respond.

Mr. Boner thought he could get one over on me, since I was newly separated and in a vulnerable state. I felt a bit inept and knew I needed to learn how to stand my ground. Maybe he treated all women like this?

I had to learn from the situation and move forward. It took several days to process.

Now, every time I pass a Bonefish Grill, I think of it as "Bonerfish Grill."

Red Flags
- ❖ Pushy, vile, and disrespectful.
- ❖ Drunken misogynist.

Insights and Lessons Learned
- ❖ Get up and leave! Don't put up with pushy, vile, drunken, disrespectful, inexcusable, misogynistic behavior.

November

Mr. Whip: *The Single Guy*

I was with a group of girls much younger than me. We were hanging out in Delray Beach on Atlantic Ave, at a bar. I call it the Ave. It's the thoroughfare in Delray that goes to the beach with restaurants, bars, and shops. A very happening place. The girls decided they wanted to go to Rocco's Tacos in Boca, so impulsively, I jumped into a car with them. I felt like I was 25 again.

We were having drinks. I glanced over and saw Mr. Whip sitting amongst a group of guys. He's hot! But . . . is that a toupee? *Hmm?* He looked like he was much younger than me. He caught me gazing at him and smiled. I smiled back. *Crap!* I hope he didn't notice me staring at his head.

He's walking over here. I'd always had a weakness for a guy with a great body and an attractive face to go along with it. He was definitely a gym rat.

"Hi, I'm Mr. Whip."

"Hey, nice to meet you."

"Can I buy you a drink?"

I didn't need another, but why not? We chatted as I sipped. I was having trouble getting past his toupee, but I tried to put it out of my mind.

"We're going to Delray to the dance club." One of the girls said to me.

"Oh, okay."

"I'd like to spend more time with you. Can I drive you up to meet the girls a little later?" Mr. Whip looked at me.

"Um. Okay."

What was I thinking? I didn't know this person. My intuition was telling me he was a respectable guy, and the drink didn't help.

A while later, we left. As we got to his car, he waved his hand out in front.

"This is my Aston Martin two-door coupe."

"Nice."

We got in and he drove north. After a few miles, he pulled into the left turn lane.

"Where are you going Mr. Whip?"

"I'm going to my house. I live right down the street." *Oh no . . .*

"Let's get something straight Mr. Whip. You offered to drive me back to the dance club on the Ave. The reason I let you drive me was because I thought I'd feel safer with you. The girl who drove me seemed tipsy on the way to Rocco's. Maybe it was my mistake to trust you?

With that being said, I don't want to go to your house, nor am I going to have sex with you."

What if his toupee fell off while we were doing it? The thought of that occurring . . . well, I couldn't even fathom it.

"Yes, you can trust me to get you to Delray. You can't blame a guy for trying, can you?"

I didn't answer. *Dude, drive that Aston Martin like I'd race it on a racetrack.* He was driving slowly. I was antsy and wanted to get there.

I was relieved when we got to the club and Mr. Whip parked. He leaned over and gave me a kiss. The kissing got deeper. I went with it. Instinctively, I put my hand on the back of his head. *Ew.* I'd never touched a toupee before. It felt kind of gross and bristly like straw, and it covered his entire head. I could feel the plastic mold through the synthetic hair. Maybe I should've called it a wig instead of a toupee. He pulled away.

"I'm a little self-conscious. I wear a hairpiece. I'm only 38, but I lost my hair early."

I couldn't dignify a real response. I just said, "okay."

He started kissing me again. We were laughing and kissing and having a good time. Finally, I stopped fixating on his toupee. Time passed quickly. We came up for air.

"Shit! I forgot about the girls."

"You can still meet them."

"Okay, soon."

I really didn't care about the girls. They weren't good friends; they wouldn't miss me. He started kissing me again. I forgot about them. He moved his seat all the way back. He turned and brought his left leg over the middle column to my side. *What's he doing?*

"Pull your seat back." He directed.

He brought his other leg over. He was hunched over with the back of his head against the windshield. I was hoping his toupee didn't get stuck to the windshield and I would see his bald head when he leaned forward. That wouldn't have been a pretty sight. I pressed the other button to recline the top of the seat all the way back. He leaned on top of me and started kissing me again. Then, he pushed away from me. He yanked at the buttons on his jeans. Like a jack-in-the-box. Pop! Goes his weasel. Boing! His hard schlong was looking straight up at me. *Holy shit!*

"Put that thing away! I already told you I'm not having sex with you tonight."

Did he really just whip that out? Yeah . . . he did. I kept my composure. I didn't want him to know I was rattled. He put his hard schlong back in his jeans and buttoned up. *Phew!* At least he listened. I was afraid he was going to negotiate or beg.

"It's getting late and it's time for me to go. Please drive me to the valet." I said to him.

"I'll wait until you get your car."

"You want me to be safe, right?" I rolled my eyes.

"That's odd. My car's right out in front."

I got out and walked to the valet.

"I've been waiting for over an hour." The valet said.

"I'm so sorry. Thank you for waiting." *SHIT!*

"We close at midnight, just so you know for the next time."

I went into my bag and handed him a twenty, got into my car, and waved goodbye to Mr. Whip.

I was flabbergasted. I undoubtedly had to review, regroup, and be more aware of what I got myself into. I was way out of my element and definitely needed a reality check.

The next morning, Mr. Whip started blowing up my phone. He invited me to his house for brunch. I knew he just wanted to have sex, but I wasn't ready since I had just gotten separated, and I wasn't ready to give it up yet.

That same day, my girlfriend invited me to her gym. We were on stationary bikes when I looked up and saw Mr. Whip in the free-weight section. He was ripped. He saw me staring at him and smiled. *Stay calm!* I smiled back.

Later on, he started blowing up my phone again. I didn't answer.

Seven months later—

I was out celebrating my birthday when I ran into Mr. Whip sitting inside the bar of the dance club.

"Hi. I still can't believe you did that." I rolled my eyes.

"You can't blame a guy for trying, can you?" He reiterated, while shrugging his shoulders.

We laughed about our night together. I said goodbye and left the club. He started blowing up my phone, but I didn't answer.

Red Flags
- ❖ He deceived me and attempted to take me to his house to have sex.
- ❖ He thought he was deserving of a blow job when he whipped out his schlong.

Insights and Lessons Learned
- ❖ Be careful! Going into a car with a stranger is not the smartest idea, even if he drives an Aston Martin.

❖ He who drives an Aston Martin doesn't deserve a blowjob just because he whipped it out!

November

The Vampire: *A Newly Single Divorcé*

I was with some friends at Rocco's Tacos in Boca again. I spotted The Vampire looking at me and smiled back. *Hello. Who are you?* He was definitely much younger than me. He was very attractive. He had wavy, dark brown hair and an intense gaze. He looked mysterious.

He came over. We began to talk and hung out for a while. He was 37, divorced, and had a young daughter. He had just ended a long-term relationship since the divorce. Not only was I new to this, but I also hadn't given any thought to a guy that age who had a young child.

He walked me to my car. The Vampire leaned onto me against my car and started to kiss me. I felt intense chemistry between us. It became very hot. He started nibbling at my neck. *Ooh!* Then, he bit down harder! *Ow!* I pulled back and looked at him.

"Whoa. That was erotic." I had a surprised look.

I was shocked and turned-on at the same time.

"These are my specialty." He said, as he flexed his eye teeth with a big grin.

We laughed and we made out some more.

"I'd better go now." I said while holding The Vampire's hand.

"Can I have your number?" He asked.

"Sure."

The next day—

I was sitting on the beach with my girlfriend Karen.

"What are those marks on your neck?" She looked at me dumbfoundedly.

"You're not going to believe this. It was hot!"

I told her the story.

"You're right, I can't believe that."

"They were the pointiest eye teeth I'd ever seen and felt."

A little while later, The Vampire texted me—
Hey. Where are you?

Me—
I'm at the beach in Delray with my girlfriend.

Him—
I'm coming to see you

Me—
Great. We're sitting in front of Boston's.

"What do I do?" I asked Karen. "I thought he was just a quick meet–make out–bite my neck. Nothing more."

"Well, it seems like he wants more. Just play it out."

"Whatever that means." I shook my head.

"See what happens and go with it."

"First of all, he's only 37, and has a young kid, and second, I'm new to this and haven't been out there long enough to know how to handle someone like The Vampire. I get the feeling he just wants to have casual sex."

"Play it out." Karen said, again.

A little while later, he called and told me his boat had broken down. He showed up a couple hours later with his brother who I'd met the night before. We all went for a bite to eat at Boston's. Then, he told us he had an event to go to and said goodbye.

The next day—

He texted me—
Hi, how are you?

Me—
Good and you?

Him—
You want to hang out tonight?

Me—
I want to be in a relationship before jumping in. As you know I'm newly separated. I'm not looking for something just casual at this time.

Him—
I am looking for only casual right now. I just got out of a long-term relationship since my divorce.

Why did I think he would respond positively to that text? What was I thinking? I should have asked an experienced friend for advice before sending that message. I really needed to learn the game. I was too inexperienced to handle The Vampire. I wasn't in the appropriate headspace for this guy. We were in different phases of our lives.

Red Flags
- ❖ He wanted to keep it casual.

Insights and Lessons Learned
- ❖ I had no experience in how to handle this guy. I needed to learn the game and gain experience.
- ❖ Ask for advice from an experienced friend before sending a text that's regrettable.

November

Mr. Harley Married: *The Not-So Cheater*

I headed out to the Ave in Delray with my girlfriend Karen. We were standing at the bar at Vic and Angelo's when Mr. Harley Married came up to order a drink. He nodded at me. I smiled back.

I glanced his way a couple minutes later and saw a woman giving him a kiss on the cheek and a hug.

"I wonder who that is?" I looked at Karen.

A few minutes later they came over.

"Hello, I'm Mr. Harley Married, and this is my sister."

"Hi, nice to meet you."

A little while later his sister invited us to join them for dinner. We accepted, and the four of us sat down at a table. We were eating, drinking, and enjoying our time together. The night drifted away.

"I have to go, it's getting late." Karen got up from her seat.

His sister said goodbye and left.

"Have you ever been on a Harley?" Mr. Harley Married asked.

"No, I've never been on a bike."

"Do you want to take a ride to the beach before I drop you off at your car?"

"Sure."

He helped me onto his Harley, and I put my arms around him tightly. He drove down the Ave slowly. It was eerily quiet. The breeze felt cool on my face. He parked the bike. He turned himself around and leaned in for a kiss. I didn't expect that. He gave me no clue he was interested in me at all, but I liked it! He backed away after a minute and glanced at his watch.

"It's 1:30, we better get going."

"Whoa, I had no idea it was so late."

He drove me back to my car and said goodnight.

The next morning came too soon.

I sent Mr. Harley Married a text—
Thanks for dinner and the ride last night. I had fun.

A little while later, my best friend D and I were taking our usual walk around the neighborhood. It was our time to catch up on the events of the week.

"OMG, I'm so tired. I got in late." I said to D.

"Okay, what happened last night?" She looked at me.

"Nothing much."

I'd just finished telling her the story when my phone rang.

"Hello." I answered.

"Hello."

"Who is this?" I asked.

"That guy you were with last night, he is my husband."

"Your what?" I rolled my eyes at D.

"You better not see him again."

She babbled on. *Yeah, yeah, yeah . . . blah, blah, blah.*

"I was just thanking him and his sister for dinner last night."

"Are you sure about that? You had better not have had sex with him."

"No worries. I can assure you nothing happened. He didn't have his dick inside of me."

What the hell did you just say? D mouthed to me.

"It was all very innocent. His sister invited me because I'm getting divorced. She thought that maybe I would hire her if I needed a divorce attorney. Maybe you should talk to your man before accusing?"

I hung up the phone.

"I can't believe you just said that to her. What were you thinking?" D said.

"First of all, I'm extremely tired and I wasn't thinking. Second, it was the truth."

"Well, I think you better be careful who you ride on a Harley with next time." D said.

"Ya think? Nobody mentioned a wife. I'm going to call his sister to find out what's really going on."

"You have her number?"

"Yeah, she put both of their numbers in my phone. I gather she wanted to set me up with her brother, who's a chiropractor. She told me I was welcome to call her if I needed divorce advice."

I was perplexed and called her.

"I just got a call from some bitch who told me she was your brother's wife."

"He isn't married. That's his ex-girlfriend. She's very jealous and possessive. I thought they broke up."

"I wouldn't be so sure of that. I sent a text thanking him for dinner. She must have been there with him and read his texts."

I never heard from him again.

So much for Mr. Harley Married. Maybe I should have called him Mr. Hardly Married!

Red Flags
- ❖ Does sharing a momentary kiss with me count as cheating?
- ❖ His "so-called" wife called me.

Insights and Lessons Learned
- ❖ He wasn't married. I didn't consider him a cheater.
- ❖ Be careful of guys with a crazy ex.
- ❖ Don't give unnecessary information.

3
THE REBOUNDS

Having to write about this rebound relationship, and relive it again, was both uncomfortable and cathartic.

November-December

Mr. Sex Sigma: *The Compulsive, Manipulative, Narcissistic, Pathological Liar, Stalker with Addictions*

He was soft spoken and had a sexy Spanish accent.

"I'm from Uruguay. When I was 18, my parents enlisted me in the Israeli army."

Mr. Sex Sigma began telling me all about his life. He told me everything he had been through. He was a great storyteller. He seemed fascinating and I was captivated.

"I'm a consultant and I have a Six Sigma Black Belt certification."

What did he say? Six—Sex? I was having trouble understanding him.

"I can't wait to meet you. You're gorgeous." He complimented.

"Thank you."

I hadn't heard those words ever before, let alone with a sexy Spanish accent! That gave me a warm feeling.

"I'm going to visit my cousin for a few days. We can talk after I get back from New York."

I needed to get away from the stress of my separation and my newfound loneliness. It wasn't easy being alone after 24 years. I was dealing with a lot of shit. It was all very new and unsettling.

My cousin picked my daughter and I up at the airport. We settled into her condo after dropping my daughter off with her friend. Mr. Sex Sigma called on the phone.

"I think I saw you at the airport."

"You . . . what?"

"I wanted to meet you, so I went to the airport. I got there just in time. You were outside. You were standing there with a teenager, so I didn't come up to you. Was that your daughter?"

"Yes."

Holy shit! Did he really just do that? I always had trouble understanding accents.

"Why would you go to the airport?"

I was getting nauseas just saying it. *Crap!* How stupid of me! I should never have given him the details of my trip.

"I was dying to meet you. I couldn't help myself. I like you so much already. You are as gorgeous as I thought you'd be, even though we've never met."

He was saying nice things, but it felt very weird.

"Don't you think you took it a little too far? You're giving me the creeps!"

"I'm so sorry. That wasn't my intention. I just had an impulse to see you. I'm so glad I did because now I'm even more excited. Please come back and meet me. We can get to know each other even more. You won't regret it. I'll pick you up at the airport and take you to dinner."

On and on, for over an hour, he tried to persuade me like a toddler having a tantrum, until he got his way.

"I'm not giving you an answer right now. I'll let you know when I decide."

I was torn. My head was spinning like a top. I hashed it out with my cousin. I still had no clarity. I was lost and inexperienced. My cousin had little dating experience or advice to give me. She met her boyfriend at a wedding soon after her divorce. She didn't seem worried.

He started texting me—
I'm sorry. I'll never do something like that again.

Me—
Give me time.

Him—
I am dying to meet you. You won't regret it. I'll treat you like a princess.

A while later, he called again. He continued putting on the charm, using his soft-spoken, sexy, Spanish accent.

The apologizing lasted for days. My inexperienced cousin still had no concerns.

YES—NO—YES—NO

I thought about it some more.

I finally responded—
Okay, you wore me down. I'll meet you.

Why did I say yes? I gave in. I wasn't listening to my intuition. He was pursuing me and was very persuasive. I needed some kind words. I was lonely, and in a shitty place in my life.

The next day, my cousin drove me to the airport. On the airplane, I was anxious and fidgety. I spoke to the women next to me. She was impressed that Mr. Sex Sigma pursued me so relentlessly. Was I making him look like my knight in shining armor?

The confusion continued. The airplane finally landed. I apprehensively got off. I was sweating profusely. There he stood, as I approached the exit. His face lit up. I half-smiled back. He was fairly attractive, in decent physical shape, but was on the shorter side and nothing to get excited about. He looked older than 55.

"Hello."

"Nice to meet you." I said in a subdued tone.

"I'm taking you to The Breakers Hotel on Palm Beach for a nice dinner."

"Okay."

We walked around the grounds and sat on a lounge chair. The pool area was empty. After a few minutes, he leaned in for a kiss. *Huh?* That came out of nowhere. I felt flush. The pool boys were looking at us. One was staring and then covering his smirk with a towel.

"Let's get out of here. It's a bit embarrassing." I said to him.

"Okay. I reserved a room so we can relax, and you can change before dinner."

"You did what? I'm a little uneasy going to this room with you. I don't even know you."

"It's no big deal. You can trust me. We've been talking for over a week. You know me pretty well by now."

"Oh."

I know him? My stomach started to churn. He lit up a cigarette as we walked away.

"You smoke? I hate smoking. Disgusting habit. I've been health conscious most of my life."

"I've been trying to quit. I'm almost there. I only smoke a couple a day."

"Well, I hope you quit soon. I don't want to date a guy who smokes."

"I promise." He smiled back at me.

"I'm not really comfortable with this room idea. I wasn't planning on having sex with you tonight. Honestly, I just got separated as you know. I'm definitely not ready."

"Of course, I understand. You don't have to do anything you don't want to."

I was getting more edgy. Why the hell was I going along with him?

YES—NO—YES—NO

We arrived at the room.

"I'll go get your bag, so you can change your clothes."

He came back a couple minutes later.

"Go get changed."

I went into the bathroom and changed.

"You look gorgeous."

"Thank you."

We left the room. He lit up another cigarette. That's TWO. I hated smoker's breath.

I ordered a drink to calm myself down. I wasn't much of a drinker, but at that point, I needed to squelch my anxiety. I was also a lightweight, so I had to be careful. He ordered a soda. *A soda? Hmm?*

"Aren't you going to have a drink?" I asked.

"No, I'm an alcoholic. I haven't had a drink in a few years."

Smoker? Alcoholic? Was there anything else that he wanted to tell me? He changed the subject and kept on reinforcing our connection and telling me how beautiful I was. I liked what I heard. It felt good. The alcohol was easing my nerves.

We finished dinner and left the restaurant. As we walked outside, he lit up again. That's THREE. We entered the room. He went into the bathroom to gargle. I started feeling apprehensive again. My radar was on high alert, but I felt paralyzed.

He sat me on the bed. He started to kiss me. The next thing I knew, I was being seduced. I had no idea what had happened. I felt as if I had an outer body experience. Was that me there in the bed with him? I could barely remember the act, it happened so fast, but it did, and it was too late to turn back. I felt numb. He lit up again. That's FOUR! Into the bathroom to gargle.

I felt tainted and dirty. I didn't sleep for a minute. My stomach was wrapped in knots. *OMG!* How did that happen? I let it happen. I had no answers. I was disgusted with myself and wanted out. It was the first time I'd had sex with a guy since I got separated. I felt deflowered all over again, not really deflowered, but sickened. I went home and threw my smelly, smoky clothes in the wash.

A few days later, he convinced me to drive up and see him again. I knew I shouldn't go, but I went along with his manipulation. He kept telling me what I wanted to hear. It felt good.

YES—NO—YES—NO

On my drive up to his townhouse, I did deep breathing exercises. In with a breath, out through the nose, in with a breath. Next, I sang show tunes— something my therapist taught me to do when I was anxious. *Oklahoma, where the wind comes sweepin' down the plain . . . Oklahoma.* Rotating for 45 minutes during the entire drive. I was hyperventilating, but I never turned around to drive home.

Once or twice a week, for three weeks, I drove to Palm Beach Gardens to his "nothing special" townhouse, that he said cost "the big bucks." We would have sex, go to lunch, and then have "nothing special" very-quick-and-over-with, sex again. He would light up many times in the couple hours I was with him. What happened to quitting? *LIAR!* He also lied about his townhouse being expensive. I have always kept abreast of the real estate market. It wasn't about the value of the townhouse; it was the fact that he was lying to impress me. To impress himself.

He was very predictable. Have sex—light up—gargle. Go to lunch. Light up—gargle—have sex—light up—gargle. I then realized he also had a sex addiction.

He took me to fine restaurants. He was always rude to the waitstaff, and I was deplored by his behavior.

He had a teensy-weensy schlong. The smallest, I'd ever seen. He would huff and puff to catch his breath afterwards. Huff and puff—huff and puff. It was repulsive.

He was going out of his way to make me feel wanted, which I hadn't felt in years. I knew he was manipulating me; I didn't want to be alone. He was saying all the things I needed to hear. He was sucking me in, and I recognized it. I allowed him to have an unusual hold on me.

I decided to look him up online. Why didn't I do it sooner? I'm a trusting person.

I went to his townhouse again, a few days later.

"It says online, you're 60, not 55. Let me see your driver's license."

I saw his license on the coffee table, but before I could grab it, he took it and put it in his wallet.

"No. Why don't you believe me? Everything I've told you about myself is the truth."

You just hid your license.

"I'm not sure about that. Things aren't adding up for me."

He told me an elaborate story about how his parents lied about his age to get him inducted into the Israeli Army. His stories seemed far-fetched. I chalked it up to his narcissistic behavior, making himself feel good in some way.

"I don't think I can do this with you anymore." I stated.

"Please don't do this. I have fallen for you. I don't know what I would do without you. Please! Go away with me overnight on Saturday. I want to treat you like the princess you are." On and on . . . He pleaded.

"I need to think. I'm torn."

"Please don't give up on me . . . please." He begged.

Something seemed way off. I'd just set up a date with another guy named **Uncle Scooter** for the following week. Uncle Scooter told me he had a hotel timeshare and would be there at the same time as me and Mr. Sex Sigma. I distinctly remembered the name of the hotel. What if I ran into Uncle Scooter while I was there with Mr. Sex Sigma? I was alarmed. I had an eerie feeling this was no coincidence. What's going on here?

YES—NO—YES—NO

Mr. Sex Sigma convinced me to meet him. He was very persuasive, and relentless.

I was in a paranoid state as we walked through the hotel lobby. The weather was blustery, and it rained all day, so we stayed in the hotel room and had sex numerous times in between meals. Did he take a little blue pill? He'd light up—gargle—we'd have sex. Repeat! We did nothing else.

I was feeling distressed and went to the gym. When I got back, he was sulking. He said he puked from the antacid I gave him. He started accusing me of setting up a date with another guy, **Karate Kid**, which was true, but I wouldn't admit to it. How did he know all this shit? I was in a panic and wanted out. I needed to leave, but I stayed.

We went to dinner. He again was extremely curt to the staff and surprisingly, to me. He claimed he felt sick, and the service sucked. I tried calming him down, but I had no success.

"I love you and won't share you with anyone else. Nobody will treat you the way I do. I treat you like a princess."

"You love me? I've only known you for barely three weeks. We've been together only five or six times. We only spend a couple of hours together. This isn't working for me."

He continued rambling on, telling me more crap. I didn't believe any of it. I should've left at that point. I had no ability to say NO to people. I was a YES girl. I was a pleaser. That had to change.

I stayed the night. He was cold as ice. BIG MISTAKE! The next morning, we had a 20 second cold-blooded fuck. He barely got hard. It was his "I'll show you. I know you are leaving me" (fuck) for the last time. Afterwards, I felt filthy and the sight of him disgusted me.

As I emptied out the safe, he said, "you know you should never use your social security number for the safe."

How did he know? He was really scaring me! I had to get out of there ASAP! I was freaking out.

"I'm going to yoga now."

I got out of there. Mr. Sex Sigma began texting me. I ignored him and went to the yoga studio. I was in desperate need of balancing my brain and my chakras.

I suspected he hacked into my phone because he knew way too much. I felt as if he was stalking me and watching my every move. I couldn't shake it. The whole experience, which lasted barely three weeks, was very traumatizing. Luckily, I was strong enough to break away before I really got sucked into his bullshit.

He kept on texting and calling nonstop, but I wouldn't answer. I moved forward.

A month or so later, the phone rang.

"I found a pearl earring under my bed. Is it yours?"

I heard his Spanish accent. *Oh shit!* Why didn't I look before answering my phone?

"Nope. I don't own pearl earrings. Must be someone else's. I have to go now, bye." I hung up.

Did he think his little ploy would make me jealous? Nope! I was a little unnerved, so I put "The Stalker" in my contacts with his name.

NO—NO—NO—NO

He called for months. He was unrelenting. I never answered.

Red Flags
* Predatory behavior.
* Compulsive. Who goes to the airport to see me before setting up a date? He did.
* Narcissistic. It was all for his gratification.
* Possessive. Thinking he owned me and demanding my total attention.
* Manipulative. Told me everything I wanted to hear.
* Pathological liar and sociopathic tendencies.
* Rude.
* Addictions.
* I felt as if I was being stalked.

Insights and Lessons Learned
* Stay away from predators. They are dangerous; and experts at taking advantage of women. Not only vulnerable women. Should I have put divorced on

my dating profile instead of separated? Probably, but it might have not mattered.

❖ Stay away from compulsive guys. Don't give unnecessary information.

❖ Stay away from narcissists. It's all about them.

❖ Stay away from possessive guys. Don't let anybody think they own you.

❖ Stay away from manipulators. They will tell you everything you need to hear.

❖ Stay away from pathological liars and sociopaths.

❖ Rudeness is unacceptable.

❖ Stay away from guys with addictions.

❖ Stay away from stalkers.

❖ Set boundaries! Don't get sucked into saying yes when you should say NO.

❖ I never let him come to my house. At least, I listened to my intuition in that respect, but that was not enough.

December-February

Uncle Scooter: *The Never Married*

The phone rang.

"Hi, how's your day going? I'm calling to confirm for tomorrow night."

His voice sounded familiar, but I couldn't remember who he was.

"I'm doing great. How about you?"

"I'm excited for our date tomorrow night."

"Absolutely, I'm looking forward to it."

Tomorrow night? My brain wasn't firing on any cylinders. *Think . . . think . . .*

"I hope you don't mind meeting up in Wellington. I'm working late."

Oh yeah, now I remember.

"Sure, I can drive up there, Uncle Scooter."

It was time to get out from under Mr. Sex Sigma for good and move on. I sensed him stalking me, like a cat stalking a mouse. I needed a distraction from Mr. Sex Sigma, and Uncle Scooter seemed good-humored.

I looked around after locking my car. I put on my carefree date-face and walked into the upscale restaurant. I saw him standing on the far side of the bar holding his drink. He held it up and nodded. Did he gain several pounds since posting those pics? He also looked a few years older.

I tilted my head slightly to the side, planted a smile on my face, and said, "hi."

"Nice to meet you. Would you like a drink?"

"I don't know, would I? Maybe half a drink."

"That's a funny comment. Come on, have one."

"Okay. I'll have a Ketel One with a splash of cranberry, thanks."

"I'll be right back."

He went to the bar.

"Cheers." He held up his drink. "How was your day?"

"Great. I had a lot to do today."

I was fibbing. I was far from great. I spent my day looking over my shoulder.

"How about you, how'd your day go?"

"My day is always busy. I'm a sales Manager and it's always something with my reps and my job."

He told me more about his career. I wasn't in the mood to get into my separation bullshit, so I only told him the basics. Besides, it was only a first date. I learned a lesson to not reveal too much.

"I decided not to go to my timeshare last weekend. It was too nasty outside."

Thank goodness.

"Oh yeah. The weather was horrible."

"As I told you, I just moved to Florida. I bought a house across the street. I wanted to get out of the cold and since I can work remotely, I thought maybe I would find a good girl here. I never found one in upstate New York."

"That's too bad. Yeah, the weather is great here in the wintertime. Except for last weekend. Hurricane season lasted a little longer this year."

We had a pleasant night. He seemed like a good guy with an upbeat personality. He was not that interesting but was personable.

We left the restaurant. I inspected the parking lot like a deer in headlights. Was Mr. Sex Sigma waiting for me out there? I stood close to Uncle Scooter.

"I'd like to see you again. How's Saturday night for dinner?" Uncle Scooter held my hand.

"I'd like that." I smiled back.

He leaned in to give me a kiss. He put his arms around me and drew me in further. He was swirling his very rigid tongue in a forceful, fast motion. Aggressive kissing wasn't my style. I was a bit turned off, but I chalked it up to a first kiss.

A couple of days later, he called on the phone.

"I picked a special place for our Saturday night date. Meet me at 7:00."

He was putting in some effort. I was impressed.

I parked across the street from the restaurant. I locked my car, looked around, and scurried in. I felt the looming presence of Mr. Sex Sigma, who continually called and texted. I couldn't shake the feeling and was on edge.

The restaurant had an artsy feel with interesting paintings, dimmed lighting, and eccentric chandeliers. There were overstuffed chairs and love seats with cocktail tables in front of the seating area to dine on. Each section was dedicated to a separate group of people. It made for an intimate, sexy dining experience, and I liked the feel of the place already.

Even with the wonderful atmosphere, I felt it getting ruined by my all-consuming, sabotaging thoughts of Mr. Sex Sigma. As we sipped our drinks at the bar waiting for the next area to become available, I started talking, and tried not to stare out the window for Mr. Sex Sigma.

"I'm sorry. I'm very panicky tonight. I recently broke up with a guy who I fear is stalking me. I feel like he is right outside that big window spying on us. I needed to get that out! I hope you don't think I'm cray cray?"

He held my arms and turned me away from the window. He looked straight into my eyes.

"I'll make sure you're safe. Don't worry."

"Okay, thanks. I appreciate that."

"I had a stalker for a year. She would call and when I said hello, there would be silence. She kept doing it. She was incessant."

"You're kidding me, right?"

"Nope. I finally called the federal authorities when the local authorities didn't do anything about her."

"Wow, that's crazy!"

We chuckled at the whole scenario. I felt more at ease. I started to focus my attention on him instead of that big window.

We were seated at a loveseat. I sat next to him with my back to the window.

"I love the feel of this place. Thanks for going out of your way to find it," I said.

"Of course." He held my hand.

We sipped our drinks and laughed about our dating incidents. Mine so far were few.

"I've been on those sites since day one," Uncle Scooter said.

"Day one, and no real relationships? You never got married?"

"No, I never found the one."

He was 47 and still hadn't found "the one?" He seemed so grounded and normal.

We ate several delicious, small courses. I was having a nice time and had a good feeling about him. Uncle Scooter went out of his way to make me feel special. He was very affectionate, which I liked.

We went out on several more dates. He was upbeat, personable, and comfortable to be with. He was always affectionate. I still hadn't slept with him. I wasn't going to allow myself to get manipulated again. I learned that lesson.

I went to NYC with my friend D for a few days. The phone rang.

"How are you girls doing tonight? Are you having a good time?" Uncle Scooter asked cheerfully.

"Yup. We always have a good time in NYC."

"Great. I'll see you when you get back."

"See you soon."

"He's so friendly. I hope it works out for you." D said.

A few weeks passed. Things were going well. Every few days I would drive up to his house, pick up take-out for lunch, and hang out for an hour or so. He would take me to dinner, and we spent time together every other week when my daughter wasn't with me.

Uncle Scooter went to upstate New York for New Year's. I went out on other dates when he was out of town.

Karate Kid: *The Not-So Separated, Married Cheater*

At the end of the night, he said, "I have to get home and help my wife get ready for our party. We're separated but she doesn't know it yet."

Did he really just say that? Comical! Ridiculous!

The Art Connoisseur: *The Single Guy*

He invited me to a New Year's Eve party at his friend's house. He was a lawyer who collected expensive art from Art Basel. I knew it was safe to go, since his Florida Bar certification was on the line.

We were flirting with each other when he spun me around and put me up against the wall. He started making out with me. We rang in the New Year. A little while later, I told him I had to go. He walked me to my car and jumped in. He asked me to have sex with him. I declined.

5 weeks later—

It was Uncle Scooter's annual Super Bowl party in Upstate New York. He reluctantly invited me to go with him. He was sick with a cold and seemed standoffish. He wouldn't let me help him make the lasagna. It seemed controlling to me. He asked me to dust the glass shelves in the living room. I wasn't happy being his maid, but I helped dust. I was a YES girl. Always the pleaser.

A little while later, his nieces and nephews came running down to the basement.

"Uncle Scooter, Uncle Scooter! Where are you?"

"Uncle Scooter?" I looked at him and laughed.

"Yeah, yeah, I got that name when they were little, and it stuck."

Uncle Scooter's true character traits soon emerged. The happy-go-lucky guy wasn't so happy at all. He gained weight and became a different person. He started talking to me with an unpleasant tone. It was evident he could only be on his best behavior for a few weeks before the bad surfaced. It became clear why he couldn't maintain a relationship. He also had the worst road rage, and I felt like my life was in danger when he drove.

Six weeks passed—

I was kind of done. Valentine's Day was approaching, so I stayed. Valentine's Day was the first holiday I'd be alone in 25 years. That was tough enough. My daughter was with me on Valentine's Day, so I wouldn't be able to see him.

That morning, he sent me a text—
Happy Valentine's Day!

Nothing else. Not how much I meant to him? Not how much he missed me? NADA!

The next day I gave him a Valentine's card. He gave me nothing. Is that how he treated someone he said was his girlfriend?

Eight days after Valentine's Day, he mustered up a card, took a few pieces of chocolates from his refrigerator, and threw them into a plain tote bag. I was so disappointed and hurt. What would happen the next holiday or birthday? I deserved better! I knew at that point Scooter was not the guy for me. I deserved more than he was giving.

His fast and forceful kissing style didn't change even though I asked him to soften and slow it down. His true selfishness came out in the bedroom.

I was on the verge of dumping him, but decided I'd give him one more chance. I invited him to my house for dinner. Finally, he would drive to me for a change.

It was 6:30. Where was he? Another hour passed. What, no text? What the hell! I was pissed, but there was no way I would text him. I was hangry, and the salmon was dried out. He finally showed up.

"Is dinner ready yet?"

"Yes, it was ready two hours ago. I thought I said 6:00."

"I got held up with a conference call and then decided to go to the gym. You know, I'm trying to lose weight. I gained ten pounds since we've been together. That's why I don't want to go out to eat. What's for dinner?"

"It would've been nice if you told me you'd be late."

"I was in a rush."

He couldn't spare ten seconds to text me?

"I made salmon, a baked potato and a salad."

"Are you kidding me? You didn't make a sweet potato? White potatoes are fattening." His tone was nasty.

What did he just say? Did I hear him correctly? Last week at the beach club at his timeshare, I watched as he ate a whole plate of french fries, with a fattening fried chicken sandwich that was slathered in a mayo dressing and bacon. Afterwards, he sprawled out looking like a beached whale for two hours on one side, then turned over to the other side for two more hours. I was so bored just sitting on the lounge chair and wading in the pool. Was he fucking kidding me? I wished I'd said that all out loud!

I should've kicked his ass out of my house right then and there, but I let him stay. He meant nothing to me at that point. I broke it off with him the next day.

He texted periodically, but I never spoke to him again.

Red Flags
- ❖ The Never Married. He was 47 years old and could never find "the one."
- ❖ Selfish. Inconsiderate. Life always revolved around Scooter time.
- ❖ Nasty attitude and tone of voice.
- ❖ Deceptive. His profile pictures were outdated.

❖ Valentine's Day card was eight days too late.

Insights and Lessons Learned

❖ Beware of The Never Married. His expectations far exceeded with the little he had to offer.
❖ Don't put up with selfish and inconsiderate behavior.
❖ Don't put up with a nasty attitude or tone of voice.
❖ Beware. It's not always easy to tell if pics are old.
❖ I deserved better than the way I was being treated.
❖ I should've dumped his ass a couple weeks sooner.

4
IS CHEMISTRY IMPORTANT?

No more rebounds! No more getting caught up with a guy for any length of time, especially if he's not a good match, and has undesirable character or behavioral traits. Time to try something new, dating all different types. Is chemistry important?

February

Cowboy Chiropractor: *The Depressed Divorcé in Denial*

I'd seen Cowboy Chiropractor with his wife at the same business/social events for several years and I was intrigued. We never had a formal conversation. Of course, I was married at the time, so it didn't matter.

He was tall, had dark hair combed straight back, dark eyes, average build, and was very attractive. He had a different look about him. He wore cowboy boots, which was uncharacteristic for a South Floridian, let alone a medical professional.

I always remembered him because of his strong masculine style and his wife's intoxicated behavior. One time, Cowboy Chiropractor and his wife were sitting in front of my ex-husband and I at a Cher concert. I stared incessantly at them while she put her hands on his face and slobbered all over him while trying to kiss him. He took her hands, placed them back on her lap, and held them down so she couldn't touch him again.

I was mortified. His distaste for her was unsettling. I assumed he had enough of her behavior after all those years, and that's why he got divorced.

I was happy to see a familiar face on the dating site. I decided to send him a message attempting to jog his memory of me. Even though he barely recognized me, he initiated a lunch date anyway.

We met outside at Max's Grill in Mizner Park in Boca on a beautiful sunny day.

"My wife left me and ran off to California to be with some guy. I miss her. I miss the marriage and living in the country club and having "the life." Now I'm living in West Palm Beach in an apartment near my Chiropractic office. I have nothing left."

He was talking nonstop. For the first time, I couldn't get a word in edgewise. Usually, I was the one who talked too much and didn't listen enough. He continued telling me the specifics. Finally, I had a chance to speak.

"Does your ex still have substance abuse problems? I remembered her slurring her speech, stumbling around, and latching on to everyone at those events. She even grabbed onto me one time."

"I don't know what you're talking about, she didn't have a bad problem."

Was he in denial? My bad for asking. Everyone stared at her and commented on her behavior. We all felt embarrassed for him. I'd also seen her at our kids' school one morning stumbling around with her friend during an assembly.

He continued on about his life. I had trouble understanding it all. He had no idea that I witnessed them at that Cher concert. It was evident that being married and living the country club lifestyle in Boca felt better to him than the situation he was living in now. I gathered he would rather be unhappily married living a "life of lies," than be in his current situation. In my mind, this guy was in total denial if he thought he had the perfect life and perfect wife.

I thought he was a strong secure guy; however, he seemed beaten down. He allowed his ex to drag him down by his balls, both emotionally and financially. Boy, was I wrong about this guy. All that time I thought he exuded confidence; and maybe he did back then.

All in all, I felt sorry for him. He was a good person who was in a bad place in his life, and he couldn't move on. He was depressed and stuck! We've all been there. I've been there. I hoped it was situational and he would get past it. It was rough going through divorce and people had their own process.

A few weeks later I called him.

"Hi, I'm going out with a group of friends this weekend. Do you want to join us, just as friends?"

"No thanks. I'm going to stay home."

We called each other several times. He talked, I listened, and we never got together again. After several attempts, we lost contact.

Red Flags
- ❖ Attachment issues.
- ❖ In denial about his life.
- ❖ He talked too much.
- ❖ Depression.

Insights and Lessons Learned
- ❖ Be aware of guys who are still attached and not over their relationships. Do not date them. They are not ready to move forward.
- ❖ Be aware of guys in denial.
- ❖ I served as his sounding board. I realized I could learn a lot by listening.
- ❖ Be cognizant of depression.

February

Mr. Hair and Teeth: *The Unkempt Never Married Interrogator*

As I examined his pictures, it was tricky to see what Mr. Hair and Teeth looked like standing in the distance. He seemed attractive. His messages were written in a proper tone, and he was warm on the phone.

"How about we meet at Sazio in Delray at noon? I work from home. I can only take an hour for lunch. Do you mind driving to meet me?" He asked.

"Sure, I can meet you there."

I had great expectations for this date. I put on a casual, short dress, and did my hair and makeup more modestly than usual.

I was happy to find a parking spot right in front of Sazio on the Ave and parallel parked my car. I sat outside in the left back corner. There were only about eight small tables on either side. As they filled up, I sat there looking for him. More than ten minutes passed. Was I getting stood up? I tried to see who was sitting on the other side, but the open door blocked my view. I got up and walked over. There was a guy sitting alone in the back-right corner peering down at his phone. Is that him? He looked up, nodded, and walked toward me. *Uh oh!* He followed me back to my table and sat down.

"Hello."

"Hi." I answered.

He smiled and moved his face close to mine. His teeth were humongous and were way too big for his mouth. His face was so close to mine that I thought he would eat me alive right then and there! I glanced upward. His toupee was floating on top of his head like a big, curly "Brillo-like" mess. Big round clumps of bristly, gray hair sticking out of his ears on each side from underneath his toupee. His long, curly chest hair was protruding from his faded green golf shirt which had too much wash-and-wear. He needed manscaping! He was a hairy, curly, pearly white mess!

"Are you Mr. Hair and Teeth?" I asked.

"Yes."

I was dumbfounded! *Damn!* Why didn't I ask for close ups? I smiled and kept my composure. I felt off balance when he came into my personal space, even more as he stared into my eyes. All I kept gawking at was hair and teeth—hair—then teeth. I was getting dizzy from the up and down motion. His body was so close to mine I thought his chest hair would tickle me. I wanted to back up but there was a wall behind me. I gazed at my car. I wished I could catapult myself through the sunroof and race away. I didn't know what to do, or where to move, so I sat still. I had no idea what color his eyes were or what his body looked like. I couldn't get past his choppers, the rug, and frizzy hair growing out from everywhere.

"How long have you been in Florida?" He asked.

"I've been in Florida for over 20 years."

"Where are you from? I hear an east coast accent."

"I'm from New Jersey."

"Are you separated or divorced?"

"Separated."

Did he read my profile, or just look at my pics?

"You aren't divorced yet?"

"No, not yet."

"You're not? When will you be?"

"I don't know. It's taking time."

"What takes so long?"

"I'm not sure. It's up to my lawyer now."

"How many months have you been separated?"

"Four."

"That's all?"

"Yes."

"I would have thought you were separated longer or divorced by now."

"No, that's all, four months, and not divorced yet."

I was being bombarded with questions and was starting to get agitated.

"What takes so much time?"

"I don't know."

Didn't he just ask me that question already? I was trying to enjoy my salad.

"How many kids do you have?"

"Two."

"How old are they?"

"15 and 20."

"What grades are they in?"

"Sophomore year of high school and sophomore year of college."

"Do you have two boys, two girls, or a boy and a girl? Which school do they go to?"

On and on. He was interrogating me like he was a cop, and I was his suspect. I felt besieged. I sat there paralyzed wanting to escape even more. It all became a blur and the sesame seared tuna salad that I loved was tainted by his verbal onslaught.

"How come you never got married?" I asked.

"I never found the one. I had a relationship with a French woman, but the long distance didn't work out for us."

He never found "the one?" I've heard that before.

"How long did that last?"

"It lasted a couple of years. I traveled back and forth to Paris."

"Back and forth to Paris? You were thousands of miles away from each other, really? Come on, don't you think that's ridiculous? To me, that's not a real relationship. You're 54 and you've only had one relationship your entire life? You've got to be kidding me!"

He said nothing, paid the check and we parted ways. That was one of the longest hours of my life.

Months later he messaged me on a different site. He didn't remember me. I decided to refresh his memory of our uncomfortable lunch date.

He replied very properly—
My mistake, sorry for contacting you.

A couple of months later, I re-connected with a girlfriend I hadn't seen in a while. We caught up and shared our dating debacles.

"OMG." She said to me. "I know this guy very well. I hooked up with Mr. Hair and Teeth on and off for the past three years. He's just as you described him. Thinking back on it now, well, I don't know what I was thinking." She shook her head.

I couldn't even dignify her comment with any type of response. I was at a loss for words, and I've never been at a loss for words!

Red Flags
- ❖ The Never Married. He was 54 years old and could never find "the one."
- ❖ Profile pics were deceptive. Too far in the distance.
- ❖ Interrogator.
- ❖ Unkempt.
- ❖ He invaded my personal space.
- ❖ Thoughtless. He never looked to see if I was there.
- ❖ He hadn't been in any real long-term relationships.

Insights and Lessons Learned

- ❖ Warning! Be aware of The Never Married. I dated several. Unfortunately, they're all the same, they can never find "the one." Their expectations far exceed what they all had to offer.
- ❖ Ask for new pics or close-ups if you can't tell what they look like.
- ❖ Beware of interrogators! Do not allow anyone to put you on the spot or pressure you to become defensive.
- ❖ Don't go out with unkempt guys. They should care about their appearance.
- ❖ Don't allow anyone to invade your personal space.
- ❖ Don't tolerate thoughtless guys.
- ❖ Be aware of guys who haven't been in any long-term relationships. They are non-committers.

February-March

Costa Rican Chiropractor: *The Twice Engaged Divorcé is a "Commitment-Phobe"*

We got out of our cars simultaneously. I spotted him coming to my car. Where is his curly hair? He looked taller and cuter in his pic than his plastered-down, short comb-over hairstyle.

"Hi. It's interesting that your car is a V10. Is it fast?" Costa Rican Chiropractor asked me.

"It has 435 horsepower. It's pretty fast for a four-door sedan."

"Mine is a special edition Z06 Corvette. I take it on the racetrack."

"Oh, nice."

He continued talking about his Corvette as we walked into J. Alexanders.

"Hi, are you ready to order?" The waitress asked.

"I'll have the Asian ahi tuna salad, no red onions, with cilantro vinaigrette dressing on the side, and an iced tea with lemon. Thank you." I replied.

"I'll have the same."

"Thank you," the waitress said, then left.

"I have a different philosophy of Chiropractic than others. My practice is a preventative and wellness center in Pembroke Pines."

"So, you don't do personal injury?"

"No, no way, never! I don't get involved in PI."

He continued talking about his practice and then his diet.

"I was a personal fitness trainer and certified in sports nutrition a few years ago." I chimed in.

"Okay. Then you work out and stay in shape?"

"Yes, I've been working out all of my life."

"That's good."

He continued talking about his life.

"I own a condo in Costa Rica. I hang with my bros there a lot."

"I like Costa Rica. I've been there a couple of times."

"I was married for a short time, and I've been divorced for 15 years, no children. I recently broke up with my fiancée a couple of months before our wedding. I've been engaged twice." He declared.

"Wow. I'm sorry. What happened?"

"I knew it wouldn't work with the last one because she dressed like a hoochie. She wore her dresses up to her coochie, and her boobs were always out for everyone to see. I asked her to change the way she dressed but she refused."

Then, he continued explaining the faults of the first woman he was engaged to. Was he critical? Was he controlling? Was it all about him? He didn't ask how I knew about personal injury and chiropractors. Nor did he acknowledge the fact I knew the horsepower of my car. How many women know the horsepower of their car? I didn't have a real read on him yet.

We finished lunch and said goodbye. He was a decent enough guy, but I felt neutral towards him. He didn't seem interested in much I had to say. Of course, I wanted him to ask me on a second date. I wanted to see if we could develop chemistry.

He called on the phone a couple days later.

"I'm going with my bros to Costa Rica to put my new boat in the water."

He had a quirky personality and said some funny things.

"I don't like to kiss during sex."

Why was he telling me this? It was a premature conversation, wouldn't you say?

He would call every so often but had trouble committing to a second date. I was feeling put off. Finally, a few weeks later he decided to make a date with me. He was squeezing me in before another trip to Costa Rica with his bros.

He showed up to our date all stuffed up with a cold. He was coughing and feeling downright horrible. Why did he show up at all? I didn't need him to do me any favors! I backed away from him in the booth.

"I can't stay long. As I told you I was asked to be an extra in a short film. They're filming in a restaurant down the street. I'm excited. I think it'll be fun." I said to him.

"I know, I just figured I would see you before my trip to Costa Rica."

Why? We spent a short amount of time together and had a quick meal. Once again, we said our goodbyes. I walked down the street and had fun being an extra in a short film.

A few weeks later—

He called while I was on my way home after I had a drink with my friend Karen. I was slightly buzzed.

"Nice to hear from you. You call to chat. You don't set up a date. Why do you guys even bother to call." I said jokingly, with a slightly harsh tone to my voice.

I was sure he received the message loud and clear. He stopped contacting me.

Months later, unexpectedly, I heard from Costa Rican Chiropractor. I decided not to go out with him again. It was too late. I had moved on.

Red Flags
- ❖ I didn't feel any chemistry.
- ❖ He didn't seem very interested in me.
- ❖ He broke two engagements before his weddings.

❖ He was always with his bros, and in Costa Rica.

Insights and Lessons Learned

❖ I started to realize that chemistry might be too important to ignore.
❖ If he doesn't seem interested, don't wait around, or waste your time.
❖ He was a commitment-phobe.
❖ This guy was comparable to The Never Married.

March-April

Arrogant: *The Arrogant Divorcé*

Arrogant sent a message—
Are you real, are you down to earth, or are you just another pretty face?

Did he really just send that? If that didn't get me fired up, I didn't know what could! I laughed. I could have fun playing with this guy. After all, I had nothing to lose.

Me—
Not only am I a pretty face, I'm in great shape, have a great personality, and the smarts to go along with it.

I was sure I had scared him off.

Him—
Can I call you?

The phone rang a couple minutes later. Time to mess with this guy. This should be fun.

"Hello." I said to him.

"Hi."

"Were you really serious when you sent that message to me? Do you think anyone will answer you with that arrogant attitude?" I said in a flippant tone.

"You did."

"Yeah, because it was hysterical. I had to give it right back to you."

"You think that was funny?"

"Of course, I did, Mr. Arrogant."

"Nice, I have a new name."

"Yup, I'm going to call you Arrogant."

"Well, I've been doing this for a while and I keep running into the same types: the gold-diggers, the phonies, and the mentally messed up. It gets old."

"I'm none of those types."

"I hope not, because I have a lot to offer."

"What is it that you have to offer?"

"Why don't we meet for lunch tomorrow and I can elaborate?"

"You're asking me out after this confrontation?"

"What do you have to lose? Besides, you intrigue me."

"Yeah, that's because you've never met anyone like me."

"Wow, now who's being arrogant?"

"If you can dish it out . . ."

"I get it. So, come meet me for lunch."

"Should I wait for you to ask me again?"

"Funny. Please meet me. I think I'd like to get your perspective on dating."

"Well . . . I guess I can meet you. I can't wait to hear what you have to say."

Why did I say yes to Arrogant? I had no idea, really. I've always liked a good challenge.

He didn't seem very attractive after looking at his profile pics again. There was a pic of him in a suit, straight-faced, standing next to the Scales of Justice. That gave me pause.

I sat outside Panera and waited a good ten minutes. *Where is he?* A few minutes later, he arrived in a hurried state.

"Hi, sorry I'm late. I was on a call with a client and couldn't disconnect."

"No problem." I smiled back at him.

"Let's go inside and order."

He was wearing jeans that were scrunched in with a belt, and a white oversized button-down shirt. It seemed like he had lost weight but didn't buy new clothes. I wasn't attracted to him or his body. We walked outside and sat down. It was a beautiful day in South Florida.

"You seem like you have a positive attitude about dating. I'm irritated from it all." He said, as I looked into his beautiful, light blue eyes.

"Yeah, I've noticed. I'm trying to make dating a positive experience, otherwise, why do it? I've had a few bad experiences, but I also learn each time so that hopefully I don't make the same mistakes the next time."

Oh no! He had a nose hair sticking out. I didn't have the nerve to tell him; I tried not to fixate on it.

"Yes, you have a point." He spoke in a softer tone. "What's with the name Arrogant?"

"Well, you deserved it the way you sent that message and how you acted at first. Besides, I've given each guy a nickname after I'm done with him."

"And I got a name right away?"

"Yup and it's going to stick." I tilted my head and smiled in an "I'm-so-cute" kind of way.

"How long have you been dating?" Arrogant asked.

"Five months."

"Oh, no wonder you're not jaded about it. I've been on these dating sites a long time."

"Why so long?"

"I'm not going to compromise until I find the real deal. I'm a successful lawyer. I do divorce and child custody."

Yup. Just what I thought. A lawyer. Time to put my radar up. Lawyers were not on my A-list to date. I'll leave it at that.

"Child custody sounds stressful and hard to deal with."

"Yeah, you need backbone." He spoke softly in a calmer tone.

He was growing on me—slightly.

"Will you go out to dinner with me on Saturday night?" He asked.

"I guess so. As long as you aren't arrogant."

"Funny."

We said goodbye.

Why did I agree to a second date? I had nothing else going on, so I figured I'd give him a chance. Besides, I was giving dating all different types a try and wanted to see if chemistry could develop.

A couple days later we met outside the restaurant.

"You look really nice in those slacks and shirt." I complimented him.

"Thank you."

We ordered drinks and made small talk about our week.

"I got married later in life and I have two children, three and five."

He's 49 and has kids that young? My daughter was almost 16. My son was 20. I wasn't interested in being a step-mommy to toddlers.

"I was married a short time when she asked for a divorce."

"Wow, that sucks."

"Yeah, she made a big mistake. She went back to her high school sweetheart, the blue-collar worker."

"Why do you say it was a big mistake?"

"Because she's struggling now, and they can barely make ends meet."

Was that arrogance or hurt I was hearing? Did he think he was a better catch because of his higher education and income? That attitude hit home for me. I'd have to assess that comment.

"Well, I think there's more to a successful loving relationship than just money." I stated.

"When will your divorce be finalized?"

He ignored my comment. *Hmm?*

"I'm not sure. I wish it was done and over with already."

"I understand what you're going through. The stuff I see every day is not to be believed."

"I can only imagine. It's not easy."

We continued our conversation. I enjoyed talking to him. I liked a man with a good mind. He was growing on me a little bit. We finished dinner.

"I'm going to go outside to call my daughter. It's too loud in here. I'll be back in a couple." I smiled as I got up.

"Okay. I'll finish up here."

I was facing away from the restaurant against the railing, so I could hear. It was extremely noisy. Lots of people walking by. As I ended the call, I felt two hands on my waist with a light touch. I jumped. I felt his breath on the right side of my face. I turned around. Arrogant was staring into my eyes with his beautiful baby blues. He put his left hand on my face and the other around my back and leaned in for a kiss. He pulled me in closer and kissed me deeper. *Hello!* I didn't see that coming. He gave no signal he was interested. Was he really kissing me with all these people walking by? Then deeper! I went with it. He was a very passionate kisser. We stood in our embrace for a very long time.

"That was a nice surprise. I'd better be going. Thank you for dinner. I had a nice time. The kissing was damn good." I smirked at him.

"You're welcome. We'll do this again soon."

He walked me to the valet and waited for my car to arrive.

That make out session changed something within me. His arrogance seemed like pent-up emotion which resulted in passion—a lot of passion. I got a little excited. I was happily surprised by his spontaneity. He caught me off guard, which I liked. It was definitely a first to put in my memory bank.

I didn't hear from him for days. Not even a text. I felt disappointed.

A week later, he called to make another date. The date went fine. Nothing exciting. Again, no texts or calls afterwards.

Another week passed—

Arrogant called.

"I was given tickets for a comedy show tonight at City Place. Come join me?"

"You're calling me last minute for a date tonight?"

"I was just given the tickets a little while ago. Just come. It'll be fun."

"I'll let you know."

"Come on, we'll have a good time. Stop worrying about the last-minute protocol, it doesn't matter."

"Well, okay."

"Good. Meet me at my house. I'm pressed for time. I'm in court till 5:00. I'll text my address."

"Okay, see you later."

We were standing in line waiting to get into the comedy club.

"You know, you're down-to-earth and you're the real deal." Arrogant said to me.

"That's nice of you to say, thank you."

The compliment was appreciated, but it seemed void of emotion.

A week later—

Arrogant called me for a date. He was always pressed for time.

I decided to pursue other interests. I was going on dates with other guys.

Another week passed—

I wasn't feeling anything for Arrogant. He was busy with his law practice and his very young kids, which left little time for me. I didn't feel any chemistry, we were in different stages of our lives. I didn't feel important enough.

Arrogant called.

"What's going on, you're not answering my texts?" He asked, in a slightly irritated tone.

"I'm not happy. You don't stay in contact with me on a regular basis. You call once a week. It's not a good feeling for me. It only takes a few seconds to text or call to say you're thinking about me."

"I do want to see you, but I'm so busy, it's hard for me." He paused. "What else is going on?"

"Well, I'm having some issues with my divorce."

That was a bad excuse. I was having some issues, but the truth was, I was not-so into him, he wasn't the guy for me.

"Come to my house. We can sit in the hot tub. I'll be happy to give you advice."

"I'll think about it." I hung up.

The hot tub? Really? Again, no emotion.

I kept dating.

A couple weeks later—

Arrogant called.

"What's going on? You aren't responding on a timely basis."

"Some heavy shit went down with my divorce. I'm upset."

"I've seen it all and there isn't anyone else who can understand what you're going through better than me, a divorce attorney. Come on . . . I'll help . . . I want to see you."

Maybe he could give me some advice? I definitely wasn't thinking clearly. I was in turmoil.

I met him at his house. We drove to a restaurant on the Intracoastal in Boynton Beach and sat at the bar.

"Why didn't you call me back?" He asked.

"If you wanted me so badly you should have pursued me sooner rather than later. I explained to you that getting in touch with me once a week wasn't enough for me to feel important."

"I really like you a lot." He kissed me.

Arrogant kept kissing me and telling me all the things I wanted to hear. Now? Now, he's putting in effort.

"As much as I like looking into your beautiful, light blue eyes, I'd like to be friends for now. I don't want to get into a relationship at this point. I have too much going on with my divorce."

"I don't want friendship. I want it all. You have everything I want. You're the real deal." He kissed me again.

I was in no frame of mind to debate. I didn't want to tell him how I really felt, but I should have. We went back to his house. He led me into his bedroom. He started kissing me. He always kissed me for a long time. I enjoyed kissing him, he was a passionate kisser, and a better-than-decent lover. But after we had sex, he rolled over, fell asleep, and started snoring loudly, just like the time before. I got up and went home, just like the time before. I didn't feel comfortable staying there. I felt as if I allowed him to take advantage of my vulnerability that night, but that was on me. I could have said no.

I stopped going out with him. He texted every week. Then, every couple of months. I made excuses and never went out with him again.

One year later—

Arrogant—
How is single life treating you?

Me—
I just started dating someone who I like, and I want to see how it goes.

Him—
I am happy for you. I'm still single, but cautiously optimistic.

Red Flags
- ❖ Arrogance.
- ❖ He didn't keep the connection going.
- ❖ He had young children.
- ❖ We were in different stages of our lives.
- ❖ He seemed as if he was void of emotion.
- ❖ I allowed myself to get taken advantage of in a weakened state.

❖ I felt no chemistry, we had nothing in common, and were not a match.

Insights and Lessons Learned

❖ His arrogance exceeded what he had to offer.
❖ Don't date guys who can't make time for you and don't keep the connection going.
❖ I wasn't interested in dating a guy who had young children. It was my personal choice.
❖ Date guys who are in a similar stage of life to you.
❖ I wanted a guy who was in touch with his emotions.
❖ Don't allow yourself to get taken advantage of in a vulnerable state. Say NO, instead of yes.
❖ If you feel no chemistry, have nothing in common, and are not a match, move on.

April-May

The FBI Agent: *The Guy That Keeps You Hanging*

The FBI Agent sent me a blind message. I had nothing to go on, no pics, no profile. He seemed mysterious. I was intrigued.

After I gave him my private email address set up exclusively for dating, he sent me a couple pics standing with his children. He was tall with an average build, dark-haired combed straight back, and handsome. I had a good feeling we'd have chemistry.

We met at a restaurant close to my home and sat at the bar to have a drink.

"I've been divorced twice. I have kids with two different wives. I spend a lot of my time with my kids." The FBI Agent said.

"Wow, I commend you for that."

"I'm also busy with my career. I'm in Law Enforcement."

A short time later he ordered a second drink, which was different than the first. He began flirting with me. He put his arm around me. I put my arm around his lower back and felt something popping out. I took hold of it. I opened it up and glanced at it.

"This was falling out of your pocket." I handed it to him.

"Thanks. The leather on my FBI badge is looking worn, isn't it?"

He shoved it back in his pocket. We flirted some more. He ordered his third drink, a different type of liquor than before. He was getting a bit silly. We were enjoying our time together. I was definitely feeling chemistry.

"I have to get going soon." He smiled.

He walked me to my car.

"Can I hop in?"

"Well, being that you're an FBI agent, I guess I can trust you." I razzed.

He leaned in for a kiss. We were having fun giggling and kissing some more. It was all very innocent. I went home.

He asked me out for a second date, this time for dinner. I got excited.

I met him in the lobby of J. Alexander's in Boca. We were seated in a booth by the window up front and ordered drinks. He smiled, then bent his head down.

"I'm a diabetic. I'm going to turn up my pump and add more insulin to counteract this alcohol."

He was fiddling with the pump. *Hmm?* He had three different types of drinks on our first date.

We had another fun date. We kissed in his truck. Still innocent.

I liked The FBI Agent and was very attracted to him. He had a good personality, was respectful, and fun to be with. Maybe we could turn this into something?

He started calling and texting intermittently. We had flirty fun conversations, but nothing more. I liked him and hoped he would ask me on another date.

A few weeks later he called and said he was busy. I didn't know if he was really busy with his kids and career, or what the deal was.

I moved on and kept dating. I wasn't waiting around for him to ask me out again, since he wasn't transparent.

A couple of months later, The FBI Agent got around to calling me.

"Hi." He said to me.

"Hey. How are you? Long time, no hear."

"Sorry, I was busy chasing bad guys."

"The next time you call I might be too busy also."

We laughed. He got my message.

Red Flags
- ❖ He kept me hanging.
- ❖ He might have been chasing bad guys, but he wasn't chasing me.
- ❖ He was a diabetic and drank three different types of drinks the same night.

Insights and Lessons Learned
- ❖ Don't let any guy keep you hanging. Don't wait around. Move on.
- ❖ He didn't seem interested enough. Since he wasn't transparent, I didn't know what the real truth was. I wasn't wasting my time waiting around for him.
- ❖ It wasn't my place to judge, but I don't think it's a good lifestyle choice to drink three different types of liquor in one night, particularly if you are diabetic.

April

Mr. Class: *The Bragger Had Delusions of Grandeur*

Mr. Class asked me out many times. I decided to give him a chance after he pursued me relentlessly.

He looked attractive, but I was puzzled. His pictures seemed slightly distorted. I agreed to a 30-minute drink date. I didn't want to get stuck for too long. I was having trouble getting a read on him.

I walked up the steps to The Cheesecake Factory in Boca and saw him standing outside the front door. His extreme Jay Leno-esque chin was glaring. His bigger-than-normal head, protruding pointy chin, and deep-set eyes resembled a caricature, especially with the sleek pompadour hairstyle he was sporting.

"Let's go to the bar and have a drink." Mr. Class smiled.

"Sounds good."

He gestured to walk in front of him. Mr. Class was dressed in the usual business attire. Black slacks, a white button-down shirt, and dress shoes. We sat at a high-top table at the bar and ordered drinks.

"I own numerous businesses. I have different ventures I'm working on." Mr. Class stated.

"Oh nice." I said, while sipping my Cheesecake Factory, J.W.'s Pink Lemonade.

Mr. Class started bragging about the businesses he was buying, and all the money he was making. He kept boasting and talking incessantly. I said nothing. I wasn't impressed. My lemonade was refreshing.

"I have class . . . it's all about the class." He then said, in a pretentious air.

What did he just say? Where did that come from? I was astonished that he had the audacity to say something absurd like that. He continued to brag about the businesses he sold for big profits.

I was a little buzzed. I sat with my hand under my chin, elbow on the table, gazing at him attentively. I listened and pretended to seem interested, but couldn't stop staring at his dysmorphic chin, big round face, sunken eyes, and prominent brow bone.

"I have class . . . it's all about the class." He said again and kept regurgitating more bullshit.

I wanted to joke and say, I'm drinking vodka . . . it's all about the vodka! But of course, I said nothing. And, for me who was a talker, that says it all!

My drink was empty. His 30 minutes were up. I finally spoke.

"I have to go now. As you know, I have plans."

"I wish we could have spent more time together."

"My girlfriend is coming to pick me up now." I got off the barstool.

I began walking toward the exit. He caught up and walked along side of me. I thought he would get the hint when I didn't wait for him. Nope. It was apparent, I was being too pleasant. Always my MO.

We walked down the front steps. I turned to the stairs on the right. He pranced in a larger-than-life way down two steps—like Fred Astaire, then turned around and stopped right in front of me. *What's he doing?* He put his hands on my upper arms. His intense gaze, with his beady, recessed eyes, met my time-to-go eyes. He cupped my face with his hands. *Uh oh!* I know what's coming next. He leaned in and gave me a kiss. He pulled back. He was still holding my face. He gave me a second kiss. In an exaggerated manner, he put his hands around my back, pulled me in close, and started kissing me deeper. Are we on a soap opera? Who's filming us? I felt his Jay Leno-esque chin jutting into my neck. He was suffocating me. Well . . . not really. Who's being melodramatic now? I broke away from his "magical" spell. It was no "magical" anything. I said goodbye, got into Karen's car, and headed to my next event of the evening.

An hour later, Mr. Class sent a text—
I had a great time with you. Let's do it again.

He said he had a great time with me. Absolutely, he did. I just sat there looking good like his fangirl.

Obviously, Mr. Class was using his classy pursuing technique. I wouldn't think anything less of the guy with the utmost class.

He texted me the next night and again asked me out. I had to say no because Mr. Class had way too much class for me!

Months later—

Mr. Class contacted me on another dating site— Nice dress, I like your updated pics!

I didn't respond.

Red Flags
- ❖ The bragger had delusions of grandeur.
- ❖ "I have class . . . it's all about the class." Who says that?
- ❖ Did he think he had me with that over the top, romantic kissing scene?

Insights and Lessons Learned
- ❖ Stay away from braggers who have delusions of grandeur.
- ❖ Stick with your intuition. If you know something is off, it is.
- ❖ The kissing scene was as outlandish as he was.

April

The Motivational Speaker: *A Deceptive Phony*

The Motivational Speaker traveled around the world conducting speaking engagements. From his pics he looked hot, while standing on a rock in front of a waterfall in the distance.

He was in-between conferences but had time to break away before he flew out for his next speaking engagement. I only set up a coffee date. Something seemed off. I couldn't put my finger on it.

I was looking for a parking spot when someone gave me a quick wave. Was that him waving to me in a very small beaten-up old car? It had different colors of paint where each dent was, and the car seemed to be on its last legs. I parked and sat down at an outdoor table in front of Starbucks. I was on high alert.

He came strolling up. He stood there in raggedy, faded, cut-off, frayed blue jean shorts that came down to his knees. He was wearing a multicolored faded tie-dye tank top. *Oh crap!* Who is this guy? What year is this?

He was not attractive, nor did he look like the muscular, chiseled guy I saw on his profile. He was scrawny, had a hunched posture with noticeably rounded shoulders. His severely misaligned, discolored, and disgustingly yellowed teeth gave the impression he hadn't brushed them in months. Everything about him sketched me out; he had a creepy look.

He immediately started gloating about his so-called career as a Motivational Speaker and all of his successes. He didn't even ask if I would like a cup of coffee.

Two minutes later—

> "I have to go now." I got up from my seat.
> "Why? We just met."
> I walked away.
> "Hey, where are you going?"
> "Gotta go."
> I kept walking, briskly to my car.
> "Hey. I was early, it wasn't even time to meet yet."
> I kept walking to my car and didn't respond to him.

This was clearly a total sham, perpetrated by an imposter.

Red Flags

- ❖ Posting old pics in the distance, or not real pics.
- ❖ He drove a very old beaten-up car, dressed in a tasteless manner reminiscent of decades past, and had horrible posture and a creepy look.
- ❖ He gloated about his so-called career.

Insights and Lessons Learned

- ❖ Don't get catfished. Ask for new pics. Ask more questions.
- ❖ His dilapidated car, poor choice of clothing, and creepiness was off-putting. There were too many unsettling clues.
- ❖ Stay away from gloaters and deceptive phonies.
- ❖ Set your boundaries. Stick to your intuition. Get up and leave immediately.

April

Mr. Flatbread and Flat Conversation: *I'm Not Good Enough*

Mr. Flat Bread and Flat Conversation had a cute smile in his profile pic. His head tilted to the side while holding a cute dog. I set up a one-hour luncheon date. I wasn't sure if we would have chemistry, and I didn't want to get stuck for a long period of time.

"Hi. It looks like this restaurant is out of business." I smiled, giving him the once-over.

"You didn't expect me to be this short, did you?"

No, I didn't expect him to be that short or that broad. He was as wide as he was short. Not fat. He was built like a brick shithouse. Although I was a bit surprised to be standing eye-to-eye with him. I barely stood 5'2" wearing my three-inch wedge shoes.

"Let's take a walk. There are several restaurants here." He pointed down the street.

"Okay."

He had pretty, greenish blue eyes and a full head of wavy, reddish-brown hair.

"How about this flatbread restaurant?"

"Sure." I answered.

We sat down.

"I like the pic of you with your cute dog." I complimented him.

"That isn't even my dog. I don't know why I posted that one."

"Well, I like it. It highlights your pretty, green eyes."

"It's okay. Thank you."

I felt as if I was doing all the talking. I was overcompensating for his lack of conversation. I was struggling. He wasn't saying anything. I paused. Finally, he decided to talk.

"I've had a lot of failures in my life. I set high goals for myself, but I ended up as a locksmith. I never followed my dreams."

He had a long list of excuses. He never talked about working out, which was the only thing we had in common. We finished our flatbread, and it was time for me to end the date.

"I have to go now."

"So soon?"

"I have to pick up my daughter from school."

That was always my excuse, and consistently courteous. He walked me to my car, and we said goodbye.

Later that day he sent this message—
I would like to take you to dinner this weekend.

Me—
I appreciate you asking, but I don't think we're a match.

Then, he sent this message—
From the tone of your note, I am guessing that I didn't make the cut. Could I trouble you for a critique, for personal knowledge and improvement if possible.
    a.   to fat
    b.   to short
    c.   bad table manners
    d.   bad manners

    e.   to shy
    f.   to ugly
    g.   to little BS
    h.   to smelly
    i.   Not enough money
    j.   Fill in the blank
Thank you in advance

I was taken aback. I didn't have the heart to answer his misspelled and faulty grammatical questionnaire. Nor did I want to be the person who told him he needed to work on his self-doubt. He was a nice guy, but his lack of self-confidence was holding him back. I felt sorry for him when he talked about his life's failures.

Red Flags
- ❖ He didn't think he was good enough and was too negative.
- ❖ He was not participating in the conversation.

Insights and Lessons Learned
- ❖ His lack of self-esteem and negativity was a turn-off.
- ❖ Stop talking. This way it will force him to talk.

5

COULD HE BE MY PERSON?

April-May

Earth Wind and Hair: *The Obnoxious, Critical, Controlling Guy*

Well, hello! I stared at his profile pictures. I was wound up. Earth Wind and Hair had a beautiful, full head of thick, light brown hair combed straight up. He looked younger than 53. I wanted to meet this guy.

Him—
Meet for a drink thurs. nite?

Me—
Sounds good

Earth Wind and Hair was standing at the top of the escalator.

"Hi." He had a smirk on his face.

"Hi. Nice to meet you." I smiled back.

My face flushed. He was a very good-looking guy.

"I scoped out the place while I was waiting for you."

He pointed to the restaurant with an outside bar.

"Let's go inside it's empty."

"Okay."

We were seated in a booth with very high backs.

"What can I get you?" The waiter asked me.

"I'll have a Lemon Drop Martini please."

The waiter looked at him.

"I'll have a Sprite."

The waiter left.

"I don't drink. My ex-wife is an alcoholic."

"Sorry to hear."

His ex?

"Yeah, well, I'm a single dad. I raised my daughter all by myself. She's nineteen now."

"Wow, that's great. I'm impressed."

There was an echo when I spoke. The restaurant was empty, and the sound reverberated. I sipped my drink as he talked more about her. I was mesmerized by his good looks. Then, the drink began to hit me.

"I have to say that dimple in your chin, it's very sexy."

"Thanks. But can you tone it down?"

"I should what? I was complimenting your attractive face, and there's no soundproofing in this restaurant."

I stopped talking and let him continue.

"I work for a division of the electric company on their wind projects."

"It sounds like a great career."

"I enjoy it."

He told me more about his management position and his projects outside the state of Florida.

"How about a date Saturday night? I'll come down to Delray, we can meet on Atlantic Avenue. I haven't been there in a real long time."

"Sure."

He walked me to my car.

I was looking forward to our next date. I felt intense physical chemistry.

Him—

Meet at 7 on ground floor of parking garage on NE 2nd Ave.

Me—

Ok, see you then

Saturday night—

I saw him walking to my car, as I was locking my door.

"Nice car." He said to me.

"Thanks."

We walked down the steps to the ground floor toward the Ave. Just as we were about to cross the street, he took ahold of my right wrist.

"Why don't you give your watch to charity? You don't need it, it's just a possession."

"What did you just say?"

He ignored me. Did he really just do that? Was there something in the Kool-Aid he drank today?

"Why don't we go to Rocky's? I'm Italian, I love Italian food. I dressed up for you in my finest black guinea tee with my black jeans tonight."

Was that some type of statement? He did look good in that stretchy ribbed tank top, and had a good body, but it was unsuitable for a Saturday night date. His tank looked like it came out of a Fruit of the Loom package. Why was he wearing that huge ass set of keys around his neck? Something seemed off.

We ordered dinner and started talking.

"Shush . . . you need to tone it down."

"Why are you shushing me? There's hardly anyone in here."

"Well, you're too loud."

He began to give me advice on how I should live my life.

"You know nothing about me. We just met. Seriously?"

"Shush, shush. You need to tone it down," he said, a couple more times.

Time to end this date now. What an obnoxious asshole. I should have gotten up and left already.

"I have to go now. My kids are at home."

I was too nice as usual; my kids didn't need me. As we walked toward the parking lot, he started giving me advice on how I needed to change. Who the hell did he think he was? I couldn't wait to be rid of him.

I started crying on the way home. I couldn't believe I let this guy affect me. It felt horrible. The last thing I needed in my life was a guy like him to make me feel like shit.

The next day—

    Earth Wind and Hair texted me—
    Got back with my girlfriend, take care

    I didn't respond.

A month later—

    Earth Wind and Hair texted me—
    how r u?

    Me—
    Good

    Him—
    What r you up to tonight?

    Me—
    Why?

    Him—
    Can we go out as friends?

    Me—
    Why?

    Him—
    I want to apologize.

    Me—
    I'll let u know

I thought about it for a few hours and then decided I would let him apologize. Besides, I wouldn't let him get away with the same shit he pulled the last time. I figured out his power play and was ready for him. I'd be in control this time. I wanted retaliation.

A few hours later I texted him—
I'll meet you, but only as friends

We met at Rocky's in the lobby. I suggested sitting on the big sofa by the front door so that we would be isolated from the main dining room, especially if I got loud this time.

"I want to apologize. I blew you off because I got back with my bipolar girlfriend who had substance abuse issues. I should have known better after having an alcoholic wife. The relationship became volatile, and I finally broke it off. I shouldn't have kept going back."

"Why did you?"

"I guess it was easy."

That told me even more about his character. He leaned in and kissed me. I pulled back.

"Why did you kiss me? What happened to meeting as friends?"

"I don't know, I felt the urge to kiss you. I've missed you."

"You missed me because? We had one excruciating date. You were obnoxious and treated me like shit. I came only as friends because you said you wanted to apologize. I didn't quite get an apology for the shushing and telling me how I should change."

"Well, I still think you need to tone it down, slow down, and change things in your life."

"Really? You know nothing about me. We're strangers. You're making assumptions. If you really wanted to get to know me, you might ask questions instead of being critical and telling me what to do."

"I hear you. I'll slow it down."

"Thanks."

"Let's take a ride to the beach."

It was early, so I figured, why not. He drove down the street and parked his car. We took a walk by the beach. Then, out of nowhere, he bent down and kissed me.

"Come to my place in Jupiter. I want to be with you. Just to let you know, I need to take Viagra."

Thanks for sharing, dude; but no thanks!

"Sorry, that's not gonna happen. Can you please drop me off at my car?"

"You need to tone it down, slow down, and smell the roses."

"Do you know why you need to take Viagra?" I looked at him, rolling my eyes. "Maybe it's you that has the emotional problems? And maybe you shouldn't go out with mentally ill women who have addictions. Maybe you need to get it together and change things in your life."

He had a surprised look on his face.

"Okay, I heard you."

"Good."

You dumbass!

"Well, I've been having some struggles. I might have to foreclose on my house and claim bankruptcy. I could really use some help."

"Drop me off at my car now please."

You piece of shit! His statement didn't dignify any response. I should've said: Gee dude, had I sold my watch rather than giving it to charity like you ordered, I would've had some extra cash to give you. Oh, so sorry I can't help you. You have a lot of nerve bringing up your financial problems to me, dude.

I would never let any guy shush me, put me down, or tell me how I needed to change.

He texted me several times. I didn't answer. He kept texting. Obviously, he didn't get the hint.

Then, Earth Wind and Hair sent this text—
Are you giving me the blow off?

Me—
Yeah, I'm giving you the royal blow off!

Instead of calling him Earth Wind and Hair, I should have called him—Mr. Shush Tone it Down and Change.

Red Flags
❖ Obnoxious. Critical. Controlling.
❖ Prior relationships with women who had substance abuse issues and mental illness.
❖ He seemed like a user. Did he think he could get over on me when he asked for financial help?

Insights and Lessons Learned
❖ Stay away from obnoxious, critical, controlling guys.
❖ His relationships with women who have substance abuse issues and mental illness were more signs to avoid these types of guys.

❖ I certainly wasn't giving to his favorite charity: The Earth Wind and Hair foundation! No freaking way!

❖ NO REVISITS! People don't change.

May

Mr. All-Around-Town: *The Relentless, Antagonistic, Desperate Guy*

After months of dating, I hadn't met the man of my dreams yet. I was still on my mission. Would it be Mr. All-Around-Town? He was extremely attractive. I knew we'd have chemistry.

> Him—
> Meet me for coffee at Panera

> Me—
> I'm pressed for time.

> Him—
> There's nothing like the present, is there? Meet me at 2:00

An hour later, I met Mr. All-Around-Town at Panera. He was sitting outside at a table. His face lit up. *He likes what he sees.* I smiled back at him.

He's wearing a tank top. Well, at least it's not a Fruit of the Loom, and it is afternoon. Is he trying to show off his shoulders and biceps? He does have a good upper body. I sat down on the bench next to him. There was only one long curved seat at the round table.

"You're so pretty."

He was staring at me with the biggest smile on his face.

"Thank you."

"You're so cute. Oh my god, I could eat you up."

His dark brown eyes begged to consume me.

"Thank you for the compliments."

"Wow, I can't believe it. You're just my type. How lucky am I?"

He acted like a cat ready to pounce.

"How come you've been rejecting me for months?"

Rejecting him?

"I'm sorry?"

I took a breath. *Think, think! Come on! Think!*

"Yeah, I've asked you out a few times."

"Really?"

Think harder.

"Multiple times."

"Oh, crap. It just hit me. Now I remember why I said no to you. You dated Melissa, one of my best friends, a couple of years ago."

"I'm not sure who you mean."

"The tall red head, with fair skin. She has a young son, is funny and outgoing and lives in south Boca."

"I vaguely remember her."

"I think she said you went out for a couple of months."

I've dated a lot of women all around town."

"Seriously. I can't believe you barely remember her?"

"Like I said, I've been all around town and dated everyone, except you. Ha! I think we'd hit it off."

"You do?"

"Yeah. I've been wanting to meet you for months. What does it matter if I went out with your girlfriend?"

"Girl code. She's one of my best friends."

"That's ridiculous."

He leaned in for a kiss. I pulled away. He gave me a bewildered glare.

"What's the problem?"

"We just met. I think it's untimely for you to kiss me. And you were in a relationship with my girlfriend Melissa."

"I like you, so I want to kiss you. And . . . I'm looking to be in a relationship and get married again soon."

"You don't even know me. Please don't kiss me."

He started getting cocky about all the people he knew, all around town. I knew a lot of those people, and I was getting a sense I would get an ear full about him. Besides, it was my bad for forgetting who he was and going out with him on the spur of the moment.

He leaned in for a kiss again. I leaned back.

"Seriously? Did you really just do that? Didn't we just have this discussion a couple of minutes ago?"

"I don't see what the big deal is."

He became agitated. He started disparaging his ex-wife about the ongoing court case he had with her.

"I have to go now," I said politely.

Enough with my politeness.

"Why do you have to leave so soon, you just got here?"

"I told you I was pressed for time when you messaged me, but you insisted I meet you right away."

"Yeah, because you finally said yes to me."

"Oh. Well, I have to pick up my daughter from school now."

I stood up. He stood up. He was much taller and broader than expected. He tagged along side of me. I reached for my car door. Mr. All-Around-Town took my arm and turned me around to face him. He bent way down and engulfed me in his arms, lifting me off the ground. He was squeezing me tightly. He stuck his tongue in my mouth in a vigorous circular motion. Around, around, around, his head moved like vinyl on a turntable. I pulled away from his mouth.

"Please put me down. I need to go."

I got in my car and drove away.

Later that night—

Mr. All-Around-Town sent a text—
Hi there, have a good night. Let's get together again. When are you available?

I didn't respond.

The next day—

He sent me an email instead of a text—
i guess u changed ur mind since u did not respond to my text abt getting together again?

I thought about it, then decided I'd respond to him since he didn't get the hint when I didn't answer him the first time.

Me—
Hi. Sorry, I'm not ready to be in a relationship. I need to go through the process. It was nice meeting you. Good luck in your search.

Mr. All-Around-Town—
Gee, thx 4 saving me the time & effort with an older cougar lookin for something that just ain't there LMAO.

That just backfired on me. So antagonistic! I had to stop being so pleasant. I didn't respond.

I called my girlfriend Melissa.
"You were in a relationship with Mr. All-Around-Town, correct?"
"Yes, I went out with him for 6 weeks or so. He was cray-cray, aggressive and desperate to get married right away?"
"Crap, I went out with him yesterday for a quick coffee. OMG, he was exactly what you just said."
"Didn't you remember me telling you not to go out with him after you showed his pics to me?"
"Yeah, my bad. It was months ago, and it was too late once I sat down. Then, he jogged my memory. What can I say? I have Sometimer's disease." We laughed.
I read the emails to her that he sent me.
"I can't believe he called you a cougar, you're only four years older than him." Melissa quipped.

A month later—

I ran into Mr. All-Around-Town sitting outside a bagel café.

"Hi, OMG, your pooch is so cute, how are you?" I petted the puppy.

"Great. I'm in love. I'm getting engaged soon." He was gleaming.

"Congrats. How long have you been dating this new love?"

"A couple of weeks."

"That was fast." I smiled.

"We're in love. I can't wait to marry her."

A month later—

I ran into him again at the same bagel place.

"Hi, how are you?" I petted the puppy.

"I broke up with her."

"What happened?"

"She sucked in bed."

"Really? I'm sorry to hear. Did you try to work on the sex together? You barely knew each other."

"Nope . . . on to the next. Speaking of which, why don't you go out with me again?"

"I was being honest, when I told you I wasn't ready to be in a long-term relationship."

I lied. Once again, I was being cordial. I wanted to keep the peace with the antagonistic, desperate guy.

Red Flags
- ❖ He dated my girlfriend.
- ❖ Relentless. Desperate.
- ❖ Antagonistic.
- ❖ He took rejection personally.

Insights and Lessons Learned

- ❖ Girl code—never go out with your girlfriend's throwaways! She broke up with him for a reason.
- ❖ Stay away from relentless and desperate guys.
- ❖ Stop engaging, especially with an antagonistic guy. Do not respond to messages if you don't have any intention of dating him again.
- ❖ Don't be so agreeable and considerate. Tell him the raw hard truth instead of being too polite and passive.

May-September

Mr. Bring Me Up-Bring Me Down: *Separated but Not-So Divorced*

We messaged back and forth for several weeks. If Mr. Bring Me Up-Bring Me Down wanted to go out with me, why was he putting me off? I didn't know what his deal was.

Finally, Mr. Bring Me Up-Bring Me Down set up a date at Vic & Angelo's, on the Ave in Delray, for the following Wednesday night.

I walked in and saw him sitting at a small, round table in the bar area. He stood up and waved at me. I smiled back. His face lit up. He was attractive and looked just like his pics. He was tall, had light blondish, grayish hair, average build.

We ordered drinks and food, then got acquainted.

"I thought you were going to be conservative and stuffy." He said jokingly.

"That's hilarious. I'm totally the opposite."

"Well, your messages seem proper."

"I didn't realize that. I don't usually message very much. Most guys make dates pretty quickly. Sometimes we don't even speak on the phone. I just go to the date. A couple of times their pics were old when I meet them, so I'm glad you put current pics on your profile."

"Yes. That seems misleading."

"Yeah, it is. Besides, the only way to feel chemistry is to meet in person anyway."

"That makes sense." He smiled at me.

"I like your cute smile." I held his hand.

"Thank you."

We drank. We ate. We laughed. We had great chemistry. I had a great time with him.

"I have to go to my house and drop something off for my boys, so I can't stay much longer."

"Okay." I answered.

We walked outside by the railroad tracks a few feet from the restaurant. He pulled me in, picked me up off the ground, and gave me a big hug.

"You're so petite, I love it."

He swung me around. Then, he put me down and gave me a kiss. The kissing got deeper. He was a pretty good kisser.

"The Ave is pretty busy as usual." I looked around.

"Who cares. I'm having fun with you. You're more carefree than I'd thought you'd be."

"Gee, thanks. LOL."

We stayed there kissing for a while longer. He looked at his watch.

"I have to go. I'm late already."

"I'm not stopping you."

I gave him my I-want-to-kiss-you-more, flirty look. He kissed me some more.

"I really have to go now." He said hesitantly.

He gave me a last hug, and we said goodbye.

I had a great time with him. It was about time that I met a normal guy for a change. He might be the guy for me!

He called the next day and set up another date for dinner the following week. I was ecstatic.

Bring me up—

He was one of the first guys I could see potential with since I started dating last November.

He cancelled.

Bring me down—

Something about a medical procedure he had to take his wife to.

"She can't drive so I'm doing her a favor."

I didn't get it. He told me he was separated and getting a divorce.

He set up another dinner date for the following week.

Bring me up—

Then he changed it to a lunch date instead.

Bring me up— Bring me down— I don't know?

I had to get real with this guy. He was messing with my head.

We met at The Grille on Congress in Boca. We were ushered to a booth and sat next to each other. He put his arms around me and pulled me in close.

"I've missed you." He gave me a kiss.

"I'm glad to be with you."

Then he gave me a few more kisses. The restaurant was packed. I could feel eyes on us. We flirted with each other while we waited for our lunch. He smirked and waved to a couple guys he knew.

"So, can I be straight up with you?" I held his hands.

"Yes."

"What's really going on with you? You make dates, then cancel. You make excuses that involve your wife. You don't call her your ex-wife. I get excited and then I feel let down. I like you. You gave me the impression you were getting divorced."

"I know, and I'm going to this time. I've had trouble in the past moving forward because I'm attached to my wife and her family. We've been together since we were 16, and her family is everything. We've been married 24 years."

He seemed sincere as he looked straight into my eyes.

"Yeah, I understand. I was also married for 24 years."

"Wow, the same as me."

We finished lunch. He jumped into my car. He pulled me in and started kissing me. The kissing got deeper. We came up for air. He waved and smirked at a guy he knew who drove by.

"We'll see each other soon."

He opened the car door and left.

He called and set up another date.

Bring me up—

I couldn't wait to see him again. You know that feeling in the beginning when you're infatuated and thinking about him every minute?

He cancelled. Again?

Bring me down—

Then he rescheduled for a week later.

Bring me up—

He picked me up at my home and as usual we had a great time on our date. We were standing in my kitchen with my back leaning against the island. He started kissing me. Then, he picked me up and sat me on the island and leaned in close holding me around the waist.

"I would love to . . . right here right now, but I don't think we're ready for this." He quipped.

I laid back on the island and teased him. Then I sat back up.

"It's a thought. But you're right, I'm not ready either."

I was surprised he passed up his opportunity. He set up another date for two weeks later. He would be out of town on business again.

Bring me up—

He cancelled again.

Bring me down—

I felt as if I was on a seesaw. Up—down. Up—down. I got excited! I got disappointed. I didn't know if I was coming or going. He was making me crazy. The worst thing was, I was waiting around for him. Totally out of my playbook. He was fucking with my head. I had to cut this off before I really got disappointed or became attached. I called him.

"Hi. I can't do this with you anymore. You make dates and cancel all the time. I really like you a lot. I thought we could have something, but now it seems like you are not getting divorced, and you're leading me on."

"I hear you. I'm going to go to therapy and figure things out."

"Good. Call me when you're really getting a divorce. I'll miss you. Good luck."

"I'll miss you too."

I was very upset. My heart was hurt, but I had no choice other than to break it off with him. I could have stayed and put up with his behavior, but my head took over and made the right decision.

I had to get over him. It would take some time because I had feelings for him. How much time? I had no idea.

I decided to take a break from trying to find my guy. I didn't want to get hurt again so soon. With those lousy feelings fresh in my mind, I decided to change things up for the summer, and move on to my next stage and chapter, "No Emotional Attachment."

One month later—

July 4th—

I was in the midst having my summer fun. I was in Atlantic City for the weekend when I received a message from him.

Mr. Bring Me Up-Bring Me Down texted—
Hi, just wanted to say hi and wish you a happy 4th! My situation has finally started to move forward, and we will be well underway with the divorce next week. Kind of a relief! I hope all is well on your side.

Me—
Hey, I'm doing great, enjoying life. I'm happy for you.

Bring me up—

Finally, he was getting a divorce. Maybe we could have a shot? I couldn't think that way. I'd thought about him so many times, but reminded myself not to wait around for a guy who didn't have his shit together. He also deceived me, so I could really get hurt.

He stayed in touch. He sent mixed messages. He said he was going to a therapist. I was hopeful. Maybe he was getting the help and clarity he needed.

Then, he stopped all contact. I was bewildered, but I knew waiting around for him was a mistake I might regret.

Two months later—

September

Summer was over. I started meeting some very nice guys. I felt as if I was getting closer to meeting my guy, but no one yet.

I heard a ding on my phone. It startled me.

Mr. Bring Me Up-Bring Me Down—
Just had the best dream about you!

Me—
You did?

Him—
I did . . . go back to sleep . . . :) Didn't mean to wake u

Me—
I'm awake now, can't sleep.

I was so excited. There was no way I could go back to sleep. Besides, I'd been on the phone with a guy for hours shooting the shit. I had just gotten to sleep a couple hours before when he woke me up. I was dazed.

Him—
Come to my place, I'll make coffee.

Me—
Seriously? It's 5:20?

Him—
I want to see u. I've missed u. It's not far from you, 8 mins.

Me—
I've missed u too. Send address.

I felt delirious. I wasn't thinking. I just went with it. I showered, put my make-up on, got dressed, and drove there. I knocked on the door of the apartment. He ushered me in and gave me a big hug.

"I'm so glad to see you. I've missed you these last few months."

"It's great to see you too."

"This is my embarrassingly small apartment."

He walked a few steps to the kitchen and poured the coffee into mugs.

"Milk in your coffee?"

"Please."

"I need to get some furniture."

I took a gulp of my coffee. There was no real furniture, only a little desk, which looked like a school desk. On it sat a laptop, and there was also a nondescript chair.

"You have little hands."

He put his hands up to mine. His hands were ginormous. My mind wandered. A couple minutes later he took the coffee mug out of my hand and set it on the countertop of his small kitchen. He took me in his arms and lifted me off the floor. He put me back down and started kissing me. Then, he grabbed my hand and took a couple of steps into the bedroom.

"Like I said, I need to buy furniture. I only have this place so my son can attend the better high school down the street."

There were three full size mattresses sitting on the floor side by side. No bed frames or box springs. Just a bottom sheet on each bed. No top sheets, no bedspreads. One narrow dresser in front of one mattress. *WTF?* I kept my composure. He began kissing me again, deeper. My mind went elsewhere. I became engrossed in the seduction. The seduction? He went limp. He couldn't finish. It was obvious to me he had performance issues. That hit home for me. And, by the way, his schlong was average in size. I was expecting otherwise after seeing his gigantic hands.

I went into the bathroom. I took some deep breaths and came back out.

"I wasn't dreaming, was I? This place needs a make-over." I looked at him.

"I told you it was embarrassing, and I'm going to rent a better place soon."

"That makes sense."

No, it didn't. Nothing made sense. It wasn't about the size of the apartment; it was how it was furnished. If I could even call it furnished. It looked like he got everything from a thrift store. He told me he made a good living, over 200k a year.

I drove to the Thai restaurant up the street, and we had lunch. He told me his car was in the shop. We then went back to his apartment and had sex again.

"See, I told you, I was good. I was just nervous with you the first time."

His performance was average at best.

"I have to go home now. I'm exhausted." I said to him.

It was late afternoon. I went home and went to sleep.

It wasn't the best decision to go to him that early morning. I didn't have regrets, but I was questioning what was really going on. Did he really rent that place? Was he really getting a divorce? Things were not adding up for me. It was my bad for not communicating. I was wiped out at that point from getting little sleep. However, that was not a good enough excuse for my not asking questions. Would I even get honest answers?

I chalked up his sexual dysfunction to his attachment issues with his wife. It was clear that he wasn't over his marriage. I was having more doubts.

He called later that evening.

"I had a really great time with you today."

"Yeah, me too."

We stayed on the phone for a few minutes, talking and laughing.

"I'm going out of town for business this week, but I can't wait to see you when I get back."

Bring me up—

An hour later—

Mr. Bring Me Up-Bring Me Down texted—
I can't believe you made that comment about my
apt. I was very hurt by it.

What a mindfuck! Where did that come from? Is
he bipolar? I just spoke to him an hour ago and we were
laughing, and he set up another date.

Bring me down—

I called him on the phone.
"Did you really just do that? I can't believe you just
sent that text. You could have said something on the phone
to me if it bothered you. I can't do this with you anymore.
I thought you got help, but I guess not. You have a great
way of getting me so excited and then disappointing me.
You bring me up, and then bring me down. I thought we
could have something. I guess I was wrong. I can't have
you playing with my emotions anymore. I really like you,
but I have to let you go for the second time now, for my
own sanity and emotional stability."
"Okay, I get it. I guess I sabotaged this one."
"Ya think? I have to go now. Take care, goodbye."

Bring me up— Bring me down— NO MORE!

I was very upset, but knew I had to dump him. Not
only did he need therapy to sort out his divorce issues, but
he also needed therapy for his bipolar type of erratic
behavior. I thought he had gotten help, but two months
with a therapist, that is, if he really went, was not enough
time. I should've known better, but I was hoping.

Two years later—

I was at my girlfriend's 40th birthday party in a small club by the Ave in Delray. I was coming out of the bathroom when I saw Mr. Bring Me Up-Bring Me Down. I got excited and started walking towards him to say hi when my brain stopped me dead in my tracks. I rushed over to the birthday girl and interrupted her conversation.

"Who is that blonde woman with that guy over there? Is she, his wife?" I whispered and pointed at them.

"Yeah, that's my nail tech and her husband."

"Are you kidding me? He's the guy I dated two years ago that I told you about who said he was getting a divorce and kept cancelling dates and acted erratically."

The birthday girl put her hands on her hips. She had already put down a few and was very buzzed.

"He's been cheating on her for years."

"Really? I knew something was up with him."

"Well, maybe he was separated at that time, maybe he wasn't. Who knows? I told her to dump his ass many times, but she always takes him back." She held her drink up in the air and took a gulp.

Mr. Bring Me Up-Bring Me Down started smirking at me behind his wife's back. Incessantly smirk—smirk—smirk—again and again. I was completely unnerved. He was creeping me out. I felt his eyes on me like a private eye on surveillance. I was so anxious; I was sweating profusely. I went into the bathroom and washed my pits. I looked in the mirror. *Holy crap! Keep your cool girl!* I walked back to where my date was hanging.

"What's going on? You seem anxious." He looked at me.

"I didn't want to tell you, but two years ago . . ."

Who would smirk behind his wife's back like that? Only a bipolar mindfuck! That's who. Then I remembered him smirking other times when he saw someone he knew. It felt like he thought he was getting away with something. His behavior was narcissistic. Something also seemed off about his erratic behavior as well. Maybe he was just lying and cheating. Why did I feel so angry and betrayed? I thought he might be the guy for me at that time. He deceived me. I believed his lies and got hurt. Luckily, not too hurt.

Three months later—

I was on Facebook changing my profile when I noticed a private message from the day after the party. Messenger didn't exist at that time.

Mr. Bring Me Up-Bring Me Down—
It was great seeing you at the party. I missed you.

Did he really just do that? Seriously? He had a lot of balls! I'd seen Mr. Bring Me Up-Bring Me Down for who he really was. Far from normal.

Months later—

I was sitting at the bar at J. Alexander's in Boca waiting for my girlfriend. The Bartender I knew came over.
"Hi. What's going on? Why are you hiding behind the menu?"
"See that guy over there with his wife having the heated argument?" I gave her the lowdown.

My girlfriend arrived. I told her the story. I saw them getting up to leave. Mr. Bring Me Up-Bring Me Down stared and smirked at me as they left the restaurant.

So much for a decent normal guy. I'm glad I got rid of him early on before he really destroyed my world.

BRING ME UP—

Red Flags
- ❖ He set up dates, then cancelled dates.
- ❖ Deceptive. Cheater. Liar.
- ❖ Erratic behavior. His behavior seemed bi-polar.
- ❖ Attachment issues.
- ❖ Performance issues.
- ❖ Narcissistic.
- ❖ He was a mindfuck!

Insights and Lessons Learned
- ❖ Don't go out with guys who keep changing and cancelling dates.
- ❖ Stay away from deceptive, cheaters and liars.
- ❖ Don't date guys who are moody, behave erratically, and seem bi-polar.
- ❖ Be careful of attachment issues. Wait until he's fully over his prior relationship.
- ❖ Be aware of performance issues. There's always an underlying cause.
- ❖ Don't date narcissistic guys. Run the other way.
- ❖ Don't go out with manipulators.
- ❖ NO REVISITS! Once you are done, you are done! Never ever go back or give him more chances. People don't change.

6

NO EMOTIONAL ATTACHMENT

It was June. I had just broken it off with Mr. Bring Me Up-Bring Me Down after his disingenuous bullshit and needed time to get over him. How much time? I had no idea, but I wasn't planning on getting hurt again any time soon. It was a shitty feeling.

I decided to put my mission to find love on hold. No more getting emotionally attached for a while. It was time to have some fun. I would start dating like a man. You heard me right. Date like a man. I would keep my options open. I would date any age group. I would pursue a guy who hadn't messaged me. I would have sex if I chose to. Safe sex. What's the big deal? I wouldn't feel used. I would feel no guilt afterwards. It would be my decision. It was my truth. It was time for my "No Emotional Attachment" stage.

For many months very young guys messaged me, but I rejected all of them. They kept pursuing me. Was I now ready to explore my sexuality? Yes. What was it like to be

108

with a boy toy? No idea. Should I give it a try? Was I going to become a cougar?

June-July

Pretty Boy-The Adonis: *Boy Toy*

Was I really being pursued by Pretty Boy-The Adonis? I was flattered. He was 20 years younger than me. I had just turned 51. I definitely wanted to meet him!

On his profile he had delicate facial features. A little "ski jump" nose, dimple in his chin, and a cute smile.

I was apprehensive to meet up with my first boy toy. Honestly, I was downright fucking nervous! I had no idea what I was about to encounter. I wasn't changing my mind; I'd already agreed to meet him.

I walked up the steps to The Cheesecake Factory in Boca. There he was, standing at the top of the steps outside the entrance.

"Hi." He smiled and tilted his head slightly.

"Hey."

You are one hell of a specimen of pretty! He was statuesque! His effeminate facial features along with his buzz cut were a mismatch for his tall broad stature.

The hostess seated us. *Crap!* Not-so-good luck. She seated us right in the middle of the room. Was anyone peering at us? I felt like we were on full display, me and the 31-year-old Adonis. I looked around. Most of the people were engrossed in their own conversations. I kept scanning the area trying not to be too conspicuous. I stayed composed.

The older waitress looked at me.

"What would you like to drink?"

I wondered what she was thinking about us.

"I'll have an iced tea with extra lemon and sweetener please."

"I'll have a coke." He spoke in a low soft tone.

"Where are you from? You have a sexy accent." I asked Pretty Boy.

"I was born and raised in Israel. My mother is American, and my father is Moroccan. I'm going to Israel to see my parents in a couple of weeks. I haven't been back in a while."

That might explain the beauty.

"Wow, it seems like you've had an interesting life so far."

"Yes."

He talked about his life. He seemed very mature for 31. He had a soothing voice and very calm demeanor. As he talked some more, I sat there fixated on his pretty features, along with his very curly long eyelashes, and sexy dimple in his chin. Pretty Boy did most of the talking, which was fine with me. I had no interest in telling him much about myself. And besides, I talked too much most times anyway, so this was a refreshing change for me. I didn't care. I wasn't getting involved emotionally.

We finished lunch.

As he walked me out, I said, "wow, you are a big guy. Especially compared to me."

"Yeah, I'm 6'1" and weigh 220."

"You're not even five feet tall, are you?"

"With these four-inch heels I am. LOL."

"I'm double your weight."

"You are."

"I have to get going. How about we meet up in a couple days for dinner?" He smiled at me.

"Sure, I would love that."

I thought he would be more assertive and ask me to have sex with him, but he was respectful. I was impressed.

As we stood by my car, he reached down and cupped the side of my face and started to kiss me. He engulfed me in his arms. Deeper! Passionate! I didn't care if anyone was looking. I was in it. He was one of the best, most sensual kissers I'd ever kissed. Not to mention the youngest guy I'd ever kissed. I was definitely hot for him.

He sent a text that night—
Hey, r u free tomorrow?

Me—
Sorry, I'm busy

Him—
How about the day after?

Me—
Sure, would love to

I answered too fast, not thinking of the consequences. I had a day to think about it and gear up, or not. I knew his game plan—sex with me. Was I ready?

Two days later, I met him in the parking lot of The Cheesecake Factory. He signaled to get in his car.

"Hi, how are you?"

"Good, how about sushi?" He gave me a peck on the cheek.

"I love sushi." I held his hand and gave a squeeze.

He drove to Lemongrass in Boca. We were seated in a corner booth and sat next to each other. It was cozy. I looked around to check the status of onlookers. The restaurant was pretty empty. He excused himself and went to the restroom. He had white linen pants on with a light blue linen button-down shirt. He had that large stature. So hot. He had a sexy, big, round butt.

As I saw Pretty Boy walking back, I noticed two male waiters standing at the entrance to the kitchen. They were huddled together, giggling, pointing, and scrutinizing him.

"What's so funny?" I looked at Pretty Boy curiously.

"A lot of people take me for gay, but I'm not."

It wasn't the age thing because they weren't looking at me, only him.

"Well, you do have pretty facial features. I love your look."

"Thank you."

We finished dinner. It was early.

"What are you doing the rest of the night?" He asked.

"Nothing."

"How about I come to your place?"

"Okay."

Did I just say yes? Yeah, I did. It was too late to back out now. He drove me to my car and followed me home.

We were hanging out in the family room. He started making out with me.

"Which way is the bedroom?" I pointed.

He grabbed my hand. He started making out with me again. Very passionate. I was very nervous but kept my cool. Was this really happening with this 31-year-old Adonis?

He untied his linen pants, and it popped out. *Holy shit!* It wasn't just a very plump hot dog. It was the hot dog, with the mustard, with the relish, with a lot of sauerkraut, inside the bun. Despite the fact that his hard schlong was an average length, he was well-endowed with triple the thickness. I was flabbergasted! It was gigantic! That might be a problem! How the hell would that gargantuan shlong fit into this small body of mine, or most woman's body for that matter? There was no way I could fit one hand around that thing, it would take two hands. And forget about my mouth, that was a BIG—FAT—NO! That would be impossible. I'd never seen anything like it. It was an anomaly!

"I don't have any condoms." I lied to him.

I didn't know what else to say at that moment. I had a box of condoms in my nightstand.

"Neither do I."

That's a relief! I was hoping he'd say that.

"So . . . we can't do this tonight." I said to him.

He sighed and looked at me with a what-the-F-now frown. I wasn't ready for what I was just introduced to. I had to breathe and regroup before I thought about tackling that shlong! And besides, I wasn't so sure I was going to after getting a glimpse of his hard-on.

"I have to go soon. I need to get up early tomorrow."

Of course, you do. You're not getting any tonight. I walked him out.

Pretty Boy-The Adonis called a couple days later.

"I think I told you; I'm going to Israel to visit my parents. I'll keep in touch and see you when I get back."

"Okay, have a great time."

I thought he would have blown me off after that night, but he texted me a few times while he was in Israel.

Three weeks later—

Pretty Boy-The Adonis called on the phone.

"Oh man, I'm so wiped out, I just arrived from Israel, but I want to see you. How about tomorrow night?"

"That would be great."

"Meet me at Cheesecake Factory at 7:00."

"Looking forward to seeing you after all this time."

"Me too."

What was I thinking? I wasn't. I'd been so busy having a good time while he was away, I hadn't given him much thought.

Was I really going to let him stick his ginormous schlong in me? I'd already had sexual encounters with a couple of other boy toys while he was away, **The Perfume Boy,** a 24-year-old, and another very young guy. So . . . I figured I'd go for it.

I left to meet Pretty Boy. I was a little apprehensive. A lot fucking apprehensive!

I walked up the steps and there he was waiting at the top of The Cheesecake Factory, like the first time. He was as pretty as ever, and so sexy! I could melt just looking at him. He had that cute smirky smile.

We were seated upstairs in a side booth. No need to see if people were looking at us this time around.

"I was having weird dreams the whole time I was in Israel." Pretty Boy said.

"Sounds like your sleep was totally off. I feel for you."

"The bed was too short. I was uncomfortable. I didn't sleep at all. I'm exhausted."

"Whoa, that sucks. Sorry to hear."

"I love talking with you. I can share anything, and you just listen."

"Thanks."

My mind went elsewhere. My stomach was doing a dance, so I ordered a drink. I took a few long sips of my J.W.'s Pink Lemonade. As he talked, I sipped some more. I was getting a good buzz when I decided to go for it. *Breathe!*

"Can I ask you a question?"

I felt my face flush.

"Go ahead."

Deep breath.

"Do women have issues with your girth?"

"Yes, it's been a problem with some women. Are you ready to give it a try?"

"I'll never be ready. LOL."

I looked at the top of my J.W.'s glass. Yup, the glass was a bit wider than his hard schlong. His schlong was almost the circumference of a soda can. *Almost? LOL!*

"Let's give it a shot. Besides, I'm exhausted, so I probably won't be at my best."

"Lucky for you I'm curious, so I'm going to go for it."

He drove to the nearest hotel a block away. He started kissing me. He was moving fast. He didn't seem like the sensual guy I'd met weeks before. His gargantuan schlong barely fit in—but it did. He was done and over with—pretty quickly.

"Sorry I didn't last very long, I'm so tired."

"It's okay, you lasted long enough to get me off."

He called a few days later, set up a date and then cancelled. It didn't matter. Once was enough for me. There was no reason to go there again. I had already satisfied my curiosity.

The BIG deal turned out to be NO big deal. Was I disappointed? It was anti-climactic, especially since I was so hot for him. He seemed to be so sensual and passionate.

Red Flags
- ❖ His gargantuan hard schlong.
- ❖ Age.

Insights and Lessons Learned
- ❖ His hard schlong was an anomaly, but one time was enough to satisfy my curiosity. In the long run, sex with him might not have been pleasurable.
- ❖ Age didn't matter.
- ❖ Be flattered if a young guy pursues you. Enjoy the entire experience with him, not only the sex.
- ❖ My self-esteem grew.
- ❖ He was kind and treated me with respect.
- ❖ He was comfortable and easy to be with.
- ❖ Embrace your sexuality and sensuality.
- ❖ He appreciated that I listened to him. Listening is an integral part to learning about someone.
- ❖ Embrace being a cougar. Have fun, but beware, it's most likely just an encounter.

June

The Sex Therapist: *An Overzealous, Desperate, Pathetic Older Guy*

"Meet me for lunch today." The Sex Therapist said.

"Today? That's in three hours."

"What's the big deal? We have to eat anyway. Are you busy?"

"I'm not sure if we'll have chemistry. I don't usually date older guys."

He was 61, 10 years older than me.

"Come on, come meet me. You don't have lunch plans, do you?"

"No."

"Then come. I'll see you at The Cheesecake Factory at 1:00."

Could I use The Sex Therapist for his expertise? I might have a question for him.

"Okay. Only because you keep insisting."

The Cheesecake Factory in Boca had become the meeting place du jour of late. Would the hostess (who worked there for many years) look at me cross-eyed when she saw me with a different guy this week? First, a boy toy, then, the much older guy. There was a 30-year age gap between the two guys. I felt uncomfortable just thinking about it.

Upon entering the lobby, I recognized The Sex Therapist. We said hello to each other. He was lean, had wavy, bushy, brown hair combed straight back, a bulbous nose, and was on the shorter side.

"Do I look better than my pictures?" He asked enthusiastically.

He stepped forward swaying side-to-side into my personal space. He had an uncontrollable tic, making his shoulder twitch and shrug, over and over. I backed away.

"You look the same." I half-smiled at him.

He came closer and I backed away again. Twitch and shrug— Twitch and shrug— His shoulders were rounded, and his head hunched forward slightly. He was getting a little too close for comfort.

A weekend hostess called his name. He turned around. His jeans had a four-inch V-shaped cutout in the back, so that they fit, because the jeans were previously too small. Weird! We were escorted to a booth, and thankfully he sat across from me.

I wondered if the same waitress would serve us as when I was with Pretty Boy-The Adonis. I was uneasy. As I surveyed the menu, I couldn't stop thinking about me, Pretty Boy, and our amazing make out session in that very parking lot just a week ago. I had no idea how The Sex Therapist kissed, but for once I didn't plan on finding out.

I felt a sigh of relief when a different waitress came to our table.

"Hi." She set down the usual loaves of bread and butter. "I'll be right back."

"Do you feel any chemistry for me?"

Twitch and shrug— Twitch and— His spasms continued.

"No," I responded.

"Why not?"

"I'm sorry, it just isn't there for me. Can we be friends?"

He seemed a little upset and tried to persuade me to the contrary. As his voice droned on, I drifted away. I continued fantasizing about Pretty Boy-The Adonis. After all, how could I even compare Pretty Boy to The Sex Therapist? It was like being awe-stricken by the Statue of David in Florence, Italy; then gawking at The Hunchback of Notre Dame. What a horrible thing to think. I couldn't help how I felt, could I?

"You said you're a Sex Therapist, right?" I smiled.

"Yes."

"Tell me about your practice if you don't mind."

"Not at all. I work with all different types of people."

He continued talking about different aspects of his practice.

"In addition, I'm an expert in tantric sex."

"Tantric, that's interesting."

I took a long sip of iced tea. I took a deep breath. And another breath. Time to ask that important question.

"I'm curious. What's it like to have sex with a guy that has a ginormous shlong?"

"How ginormous might I ask?"

"Take a good look at the top of that tall drinking glass."

The glass had almost the same circumference as a can of soda.

"Does that sum it up for you?" I asked.

"Whoa. That's some real girth. It's atypical. He can rip you apart if you're not careful. When he thrusts, it can hurt you badly. You will not have any pleasure, especially if he has staying power. I wouldn't go there if I were you."

"Thanks for the info, Doc."

"As I said, stay away!"

We finished eating. I didn't want to prolong the date any longer.

"I have to get going now." I said to him.

"So soon?"

"I have other plans this afternoon."

I had nothing to do. We walked out of the restaurant and into the parking lot. He grabbed my elbow and held on to me. He looked at me intently. Twitch and shrug— Twitch and . . . His spasms were uncontrollable.

"Have sex with me today. I will pleasure you with 40 orgasms! As I told you, I'm an expert in tantric sex."

Did he really just ask that? *Holy crap!* Yup, he did!

"Thanks, but no thanks, Doc."

I pulled away from his grip and walked sideways putting distance between us. I was a good 10 feet away.

"Come on! I haven't had sex in such a long time. Please . . . please!" He yelled. "Please!"

I looked around. I was mortified! Hoping nobody was walking into his "wrath-of-shame." I wanted to run as fast as I could, but I casually put more distance between us.

He begged again. "Please, please."

"I already told you no."

I walked swiftly to my car.

He began texting, but I didn't answer.

When I didn't respond to his texts, he emailed me nonstop. He became relentless.

I was exasperated and sent one last message—
I will block you if you don't stop harassing me.

I would catch him viewing my profile. I'm sure he thought I might change my mind and let him give me 40 orgasms! If I was attracted to him and we had chemistry, I might have considered it. After all, he was The Sex Therapist and an expert in tantric sex, so he said.

Red Flags
- ❖ He seemed harmless, but his overzealous behavior and desperation was pathetic.
- ❖ No chemistry.
- ❖ Age.

Insights and Lessons Learned
- ❖ Don't go out with desperate guys who act pathetic.
- ❖ Don't waste your time if you don't have chemistry.
- ❖ The age difference was too significant for me.

June

The Writer With 2 N's: *An Eager, Methodical Planner*

The Writer With 2 N's sent me a blind email. No pics, no profile? Why was he being so mysterious? I gave him my private email address I had set up just for dating. He sent pics and told me a little bit about himself.

Another lawyer? That gave me pause. Lawyers and I see it differently. These types of guys view the world in black and white, while I see in vibrant colors. Meaning, they are more concrete thinkers, whereas I'm an abstract thinker.

He was attractive and seemed like an upstanding guy, so I decided to give him a shot.

Him—

Meet me at the bar on Atlantic Ave at 7:30.

Me—
Looking forward to it. See you then.

I walked in and saw him sitting at the end seat with a glass of wine in hand. He held up his wine glass and smiled.

"Hi. Nice to meet you." I smiled at him.

"Hello."

He stood up, held my hand, and helped me onto the bar stool. He seemed like a gentleman. He was an attractive looking guy. Below average height, with a slender build, in a 53-year-old kind-of-way. Not nearly as striking as Pretty Boy-The Adonis, in his 31-year-old broad statuesque kind-of-way. And why was I comparing? Because—I was. Pretty Boy was still fresh in my mind.

"Would you like a drink?"

"Sure." I looked into his pretty, light blue eyes.

We started talking and immediately he made me laugh. He was funny, upbeat, and he went out of his way to entertain me.

"Wow, you are so genuine and together for only being separated for eight months." The Writer With 2 N's complimented me.

"Well, thanks. I've dated quite a bit and have learned a lot of lessons already. I've been journaling about all of my dates since date one."

"I wrote and self-published a book. You should write a book. I'll give you a copy the next time we get together."

"Nice."

We just met. Is he assuming we'll go on a second date?

"It's about my past ten years of dating. It's been a real eye-opener. And I'm still looking for love!"

"I'm surprised you haven't found love in all those years?"

"I've fallen in love for a short time, but it didn't last very long."

"I'm sorry."

"Don't be sorry. It still felt great to be in love. Love doesn't have to last forever, but I'd like it to last longer the next time. I can be alone and be happy, but I'd like to find love again. I'm not giving up."

"Well, I never give up. Perseverance!" I clinked glasses with him. "I hope we both find love that lasts."

"Yes. That would be nice."

"Why do you spell your name with two n's?" I asked him.

"To be different."

Hmm? He made me laugh and was pleasant, but I wasn't feeling him. He walked me to the valet, and we said goodnight.

I enjoyed my time with him, but I was still comparing him to Pretty Boy. The Writer With 2 N's didn't seem to emanate the sexiness that Pretty Boy exuded. Age had nothing to do with it in this instance.

Don't forget, it was summer, and I was not planning on getting emotionally attached. My strategy at the time was to have fun, and I surmised this guy was yearning to be in a relationship. Maybe our timing was off.

The next day he called. We were laughing and enjoying our conversation.

"I'm planning our second and third dates." The Writer With 2 N's said.

"Wow, I'm not up on dating protocol, but aren't you supposed to take me on a second date before you ask me out on a third? LOL."

"I guess I'm breaking the rules. Besides, it's going well so far, right?"

"Yeah."

A little eager, are you? It was one date . . . dude.

"Let's meet at Oceans 234 in Deerfield Beach. Do you know where it is?" He asked.

"Yes, I've been there."

Yeah, with that creep, The Crab Feeder, who thought it was his job to feed me my crab cake.

"Then we're all set."

I decided to stop comparing The Writer With 2 N's to Pretty Boy and concentrate on him. I would play it out and go on the next two dates. After all, it was only fair to give him a real chance.

He was standing in the lobby when I walked in.

"Hi, here's a copy of my book." He smiled.

"Nice. I'm sure it will be an interesting and entertaining read."

"Yes, you will get some real insight of what I went through."

He asked the hostess for a specific table by the window facing the ocean. He held my elbow as we walked into the dining area. He set the chairs close to each other. He took the book and placed it on the table. He helped me up onto the barstool. He ordered our sushi.

He wasn't making me laugh. His demeanor had changed since our first date and subsequent phone call. He was acting as if he was all business. I thought he would cheer me up. I needed some laughs after that phone call with my ex earlier in the day. Was it me? What's going on? I didn't lead on that I felt distressed. I had my date-face on. I was cheery. That's how I always went into all of my dates, with a happy, positive attitude.

We finished our sushi. He paid the bill.

"Let's go to the beach."

He took his book from the table and helped me off the bar stool. He led me outside. He sat me down on the sand, facing sideways to the ocean. He placed my legs in a yogi like position. He sat himself right in front of me—in his own perfect position. He was looking straight into my eyes very seriously. So, is this where his mind was at. I knew what was coming next.

Slowly and methodically, he took one hand and wrapped it around my back and put the other around my neck. He leaned in to kiss me, delicately. He started to lightly French kiss. He was barely brushing my tongue. I felt nothing. He continued. Nothing— I wasn't feeling him, and I felt awful. I gently pulled away. I looked into his light blue eyes. He tried again. Nothing— His perfectly mastered plan failed miserably. The first-kiss impression was over and done with. If he had just relaxed and hadn't tried so hard, maybe I would have felt something. Or not?

Either way, it was the complete opposite of how Pretty Boy bent down, held me tight and kissed me unexpectedly, seductively, and spontaneously in the parking lot of The Cheesecake Factory. Total passion. Now that was erotic! So much for not trying to compare the two guys.

"I have a busy day tomorrow. I better get going."

We waited for the valet to bring my car around. The wait was agonizing. I could not even look his way. I was sure he was disappointed. I was a little disappointed as well. We said goodbye.

What was I going to do? He had already set up our third date for Saturday night.

Two days later, I was in my car when the phone rang. I felt my stomach tug at me. I took a deep breath.

"Hi, how are you?" I greeted The Writer With 2 N's in a cheerful tone.

"Good. Um . . . I hope you don't mind me asking . . . should we be friends?"

"I'm glad you asked. I think you're a great guy, and friends would be great."

"Then I guess I should cancel our third date?"

"Yes."

Maybe he wanted me to negate the question and go on date three, but it was too late. I answered already. Honesty.

He was a really nice, genuine guy; but his eager, methodical planning approach was too contrived for me. I felt no chemistry and knew this type of guy was not for me. We were not a match.

We stayed in touch periodically, then lost contact.

The positive that came out of it was that he inspired me to write this memoir, and for that I'm thankful.

Red Flags
- ❖ Eager methodical planning approach. The second date was too forced.
- ❖ No chemistry.

Insights and Lessons Learned
- ❖ His eager methodical approach to rush in to make two dates at the same time, to try and make the date perfect, and seeking to be in a relationship too soon was a turn-off.
- ❖ If you don't feel chemistry, move on.

June-September

The Gambler: *Boy Toy*

It was the second week of June. I was infatuated with Pretty Boy-The Adonis, but he went to Israel for three weeks. I wasn't sure if I would see him again or have sex with him, so I moved on.

A week later, The Gambler contacted me.

The Gambler—
I want you to hang out with me in Atlantic City for 4th of July weekend.

I didn't know what to think of that one.

Me—
Not so sure that's something I would do.

Him—
I'm coming to Florida for business next week. I want to meet you.

Me—
I'll be in NYC.

Him—
What day will u be back?

Me—
June 18

Him—
I'm flying out that day to the Bahamas to gamble.

Me—
Ok

Him—
What time do u get in?

Me—
3:45

Him—
FLL airport?

Me—
Yup

Him—
Lucky me! We can meet at the airport. My flight leaves at 5:45.

Me—
Ok

Him—
We're all set

Was I actually thinking about meeting him in Atlantic City? Yeah . . . maybe. He was very attractive. He had a long, muscular, lean body type I liked. Not an ounce of fat on him! He was 29 years old, 22 years younger than me.

I met my girlfriend Karen for dinner. I updated her on my sexcapades of the week. Then, I told her about The Gambler.

"What a coincidence. I go to Atlantic City every Fourth of July. Why don't you come? Whether you decide to meet him or not, I'll be there with my family. Plus, you can share my room with me. It'll save me money." She sipped her martini.

"Wow, that's not a bad idea. I'll have to think about it. Maybe I'll meet him if he seems like a respectable guy. If I'd even call him that? LOL."

"That sounds good. Besides, my cousin will whack him upside his head if he pulls any stunts." We laughed.

"Well . . . that makes me feel better!" We laughed again.

The following week I headed off to New York City with my best friend D again. She invited me to go along with her on business trips. Her company paid for the hotel. I kept her entertained with my dating exploits. She'd been living vicariously through me since date one.

AML Guy (anti-money laundering) was a nice guy who I'd dated a few times when I was in New York City. He was almost 40, hated his job in the banking industry, wanted to find his love-to-marry and have kids with. It wasn't me.

Dusty was a 55-year-old who posted pictures that were 20 years old. He claimed he looked like Dustin Hoffman . . . he didn't. Nevertheless, he was funny, and we had a fun make out session on the street by the hotel in Soho.

The Criminal Defense Attorney was a young guy. Was very late to the wine bar, took me for Chinese food in Chinatown, and then dropped me off at the hotel.

I decided not to bother with these guys again.

The Gambler texted—
I'll meet you at baggage claim

The Gambler was standing there when I arrived. My friend D walked along side of me.

"Hi."

"Hi, this is my friend D." I smiled.

"Nice to meet you both."

Just my type! Yup, another hot, young guy. D stayed and talked for a couple minutes, and then left to retrieve the bags. The Gambler and I continued our conversation. I was feeling some intense chemistry.

"Come meet me in Atlantic City. I know we will have fun." He smiled.

"I'll have to let you know."

I was playing it very cool with him.

"Okay. But I'm going to bug you until you say yes. You know that, right?"

"I'm seeing your assertiveness. I need to go now."

I smiled at him and walked to D at the baggage claim.

"What do you think of him?" I asked D.

"He seems very nice from my initial impression of him. He's definitely a good-looking guy with a great body. You know, my husband was so hot in his prime, I couldn't keep my hands off him."

"Yeah. I've heard that for years!" We chuckled.

"Well, The Gambler is a Member of The Tribe, so I think you can trust him on some level." D stated.

"What level? Is that a good justification to spend the weekend with him? Was that also my excuse for going out with Pretty Boy?"

"You could say so. There is trust on some level."

"If you say so."

A couple of days later, I met my girlfriend Karen at J. Alexander's for dinner. We sat at the bar as usual.

"Did you meet him?"

"Yeah, he's hot, of course."

"So, you've decided to come to Atlantic City?"

"Yeah. He's been texting me every day."

"You only live once. Play it out." Karen reiterated.

"That's what you always say." I rolled my eyes.

There were two young guys standing next to us ordering drinks. **White Button-Down Guy** was eyeing me. He had a good buzz on. We were flirting and having fun. I excused myself and headed to the restroom. White Button-Down Guy followed me. As I entered the women's restroom, I felt another hand on the door. He pushed the door in. He grabbed my hand, spun me around, leaned me up against the wall, and started kissing me. I was stunned. I laughed. I pulled away.

"Okay, you had your fun for the moment. You have to get out of this woman's restroom now."

He listened and went to the men's room. I went back to dinner with Karen.

"You're not going to believe what just happened with White Button-Down Guy."

"You're always getting into something these days."

"Yeah, but this time, it was all him." We laughed.

The Gambler texted me—
I emailed you the ticket for the flight. I can't wait to see you. I've been fantasizing about being with you.

I wondered if this was a first for The Gambler, to be with me, a cougar. He seemed very excited for the weekend. It would be my first-time having sex with a boy toy.

I took my flight to Atlantic City. I headed to the hotel to meet my girlfriend, Karen. We went to the beach for a couple of hours, hung out with her family, and then went to the casino and played Ultimate Texas Hold'em and Blackjack.

"Crap, I'm getting really nervous. I've never done anything like this in my life." I said to Karen.

"You'll be fine. I'm only a phone call away. I'll be here the whole weekend if you need me."

"You're so funny. You make it sound like it's no big deal. I'm terrified!"

"Of course, cause it's not me doing it. That's why."

The next day—

The Gambler—
I got in early. I'm eager to see you. Come when you're ready.

Me—
Ok

I wasn't going to rush right over there. I waited a couple hours and hung out with Karen. I was extremely anxious. My stomach started to churn. What was I thinking when I agreed to meet this young guy?

I did some breathing exercises. I knew nothing about him, other than his name, address, email address, and the hotel he was registered at. At least I had something to go on if there was an issue. Yeah . . . sure I did.

My heart was pounding. I knocked on the door.
"Hi." I greeted him.

He took my suitcase and shut the door. He had a big grin on his face. He grabbed my hands and pulled me as he walked backwards. He picked me up, flopped backwards onto the sofa, and sat me onto his lap. He put his arms around me and started kissing me.

I pulled away and said, "hello, it's nice to meet you too."

"Yes, but we've already met."

He started making out with me again. He picked me up in his arms and whisked me onto the bed. He continued making out with me. He had me in a full embrace and started to make his moves.

"Whoa, whoa, whoa . . . you're moving too fast for me."

He looked at me with a—WTF glare.

"Besides, I'm really hungry, are you?"

That was a bunch of bullshit fast thinking. I needed to take some control here! He needed to see that I wasn't a pushover.

"I could eat, but I would rather . . ."

"I get it, but we have plenty of time this weekend. I would like to get to know you a little bit before jumping right in."

"Ok, let's get a bite."

After dinner, he wanted to gamble, so we hit the Blackjack tables for a while. I looked around the casino. Was anyone looking at us? Nope.

It was getting late. We went back to the room. He jumped right in.

"Damn condoms, I hate them."

The Gambler exploded way too fast.

"Why?" I asked.

"I can never last long with them. Even these Magnums suffocate me. I'm too big."

"I thought it worked the opposite way with condoms?"

"Not for me."

I wanted to say, dude, you are more than adequate, but yours didn't faze me after seeing what Pretty Boy came equipped with. Was that his excuse, or was it that he was so excited to be with me? I deduced it was the latter.

The next morning, we went to breakfast. Afterward, we went to the gym for a workout. We took a shower and hit the sheets.

"You were a different guy than last night, that's for sure. I liked it!" I smirked at him.

"The anticipation to be with you for the past several weeks was overpowering, but don't worry, that'll never happen again."

I was flattered that he said that.

"I'm sure it won't." We laughed.

We enjoyed each other the rest of the day, exploring our sexuality. He was great to be with. He was great in bed.

The next day, The Gambler said, "you want to get high? It'll be fun. This stuff makes you laugh a lot."
I hadn't done that in many years.
"Okay, but only a little. I'm a lightweight."

We got high—we laughed. We went to lunch—we laughed. We gambled—we laughed. We had sex—we laughed. We had a great time. The weekend was very pleasurable. He brought out my sexuality like never before. It had been in hibernation for years. Not by choice, I knew it was always there.

We stayed in touch periodically.

He called a couple of months later.
"Hey. I'm coming to Florida for business. I'm staying at the pink hotel in Boca. I have some free time in-between meetings. Let's meet up."

A week later we met up.
"I have to fit a workout in before my dinner meeting."
He got out of bed and put his gym clothes on.

I decided that would be the last time I would meet up with him.

Red Flags
  ❖ Age.

Insights and Lessons Learned
- ❖ Age didn't matter. It was just a very fun sexcapade.
- ❖ Be careful before meeting anyone in a hotel. Use your intuition. Karen and her family were there, just in case. I was lucky. It was a great experience. It turned out to be a gratifying, exciting weekend.
- ❖ He brought out my sensuality and sexuality.
- ❖ Big ego trip! My self-esteem soared.

July-August

Mr. Kosher Kondom: *Boy Toy*

OMG . . . Look at the cute Yorkie Mr. Kosher Kondom is holding in his pics. They both look so sweet.

Mr. Kosher Kondom messaged me—
Hey, do you want to hang out tomorrow?

Me—
Sure

My summer wasn't over yet. I was up for more fun.

Him—
How about The Cheesecake Factory on Las Olas at 7?

Me—
Ok, see you then

I walked into the lobby.

"Hi."

"Nice to meet you." I smiled.

He looked so much like Pretty Boy—The Adonis. He had the same broad body type, ski-jump nose, brown eyes, and buzz cut. No dimple in his chin. He did have more of a masculine look than Pretty Boy. A very attractive face. I was feeling chemistry already.

I looked around to see if anyone was glaring at us, but nobody was paying attention. I was still self-conscious of the age difference. I had to get over that. We were seated in a booth and ordered.

"The girls my age come with a laundry list of questions. They ask about the three sixes." He smirked at me.

"What are the three sixes?"

"You don't know?"

"No."

"Question number one. Are you at least six feet tall? Question number two. Do you make over six figures? Question number three. Do you have more than six inches? Yes, yes, and yes. Ha, ha."

"Good one." I smiled.

"Well, they always have ridiculous expectations. One time this girl came with an index card full of questions. They're in such a rush to get married and have babies."

He knew I had no expectations.

"You look very similar to this other guy I went out with a few weeks ago who was from Israel."

"My age?"

"31. Two years younger than you."

"Really?" He gave me an "I'm surprised" look.

"Yup." I looked at him smugly.

"My father is from Israel, interesting."

He was soft-spoken, had a calm demeanor, and seemed kind. Just like Pretty Boy. We continued our conversation.

"I'm thinking of writing a book about my finest dates." I said amusingly.

"I'm sure you have good stories, just like me. We'll laugh about them."

"Yeah, it seems like everyone always has stories."

"Yup. It's still very early, let's go to YOLO for a drink."

"Okay."

"You're beautiful. I can't believe the shape you're in and you look so young." He said, as we walked across the street.

"Thanks for the compliment. I work-out, do yoga, and try to eat on the healthier side."

We listened to the music. He was attentive and affectionate. We talked and laughed, as we sipped our drinks. He had nothing to prove, not like the older guys. It was refreshing for me. He was a pleasure to be with. Then, he leaned in for a kiss. I put my hand around the back of his head. His buzzcut felt the same as Pretty Boy. He kissed me deeper. It was very hot! He was a great kisser.

"Let's go to my place. I live in Sunny Isles Beach."

"I'd rather you come to my house."

Did I really just say that?

"Do you have condoms? I never go without them." Mr. Kosher Kondom asked.

"Yup. I want to be safe also."

He followed me home. We spent the entire night together. He was a great lover. He had great staying power. He could get it up, and keep it up, over and over. I was feeling very sexy. He was drawing out my sensuality and sexuality even more.

"Well, I'd better get going. I can't believe it's morning already." Mr. Kosher Kondom yawned.

"Yeah, our simple dinner date turned into a 10-hour marathon." I gave him a flirty look.

"It was fun with you, I'd like to do it again." He held my hand.

"Yeah, it was great. I'd like that."

Mr. Kosher Kondom seemed inexperienced in some aspects of his life, but he was no innocent in the bedroom. He was a commanding guy in bed. But—not demanding. Quite contrary to his calm demeanor outside of the bedroom. It was a big turn-on for me.

A few days later—

Mr. Kosher Kondom texted—
Hey, let's hang tomorrow

Me—
Would love to

Mr. Kosher Kondom walked into my home and gave me a hug.

"Are there any restaurants around here that are kosher?"

"There's a Sushi/Japanese place down the street. Anything you can eat there?"

"Let's go there, I'll eat a piece of fish. I'm on a diet."

"You look great. What's with the diet?" I gave him the once-over and smiled.

"You're always full of compliments, that's one of the reasons I like you."

"Thank you. I like you too."

He gave me a kiss and put his arm around me as we left the house.

We sat down and ordered. He started telling me about his trouble finding someone to have a long-term relationship with. Someone his own age.

"I believe you deserve a great girl, you're a great catch. Never sell yourself short. Don't forget that."

"I love to have conversations with you. You are a good listener, and you give me good advice."

"Well, thank you." He leaned over and gave me a kiss.

We met twice a week and had our trysts. He took me to dinner, and we enjoyed our time together. It was always a marathon. He brought out more of my sensuality and sexuality. I always stayed in my feminine space. I felt very comfortable with him. He was always respectful and kind to me. We liked being with each other.

I went down to his penthouse condo on the beach the following week. It was beautifully decorated and immaculate. The views were spectacular from all sides. I met his Yorkie. She was so cute, just like him.

I was riding him for a long time. Afterwards, he said, "OMG, look at my bed."

He looked at me with a surprised look on his face.

"What?" I looked at him inquisitively.

"It's a Tempur-Pedic! The bed moved away from the wall more than eight inches. You did that, ha!"

"No way."

I walked to the front of the bed.

"It was all you. Try pushing the bed back against the wall."

I bent down but couldn't budge the bed. I tried again. I couldn't move it an inch.

"What did I tell you?"

We laughed together. He pushed hard and put the bed back against the wall.

"Maybe I should name my book, *"8 inches and counting!"* I teased.

"It depends on what you are referring to eight inches." He kidded.

I hadn't heard from him for a week and wondered what was going on. I called him on the fly one afternoon. I was dressed and ready to go on a date with another guy who cancelled on me last minute.

"Can I come down to you?"

"Oh, ok. I didn't know you wanted to, but yeah come down."

We had a good time as usual, but something seemed a bit off. Maybe because I called him at the last minute? Maybe he started dating someone his age? I didn't ask. He didn't tell.

We stopped calling each other.

One year later—

I was with a bunch of girls and ran into him at a networking event.

"Hi, how are you." He smiled.

"Great and you?"

"I saw you last week at that fundraising event."

"I knew that was you. Why didn't you say hi?" I asked.

"I didn't want to intrude. You were hanging in a big group."

A couple of months later—

The phone rang.
"Hi, it's me . . . with the yellow Porsche."
"I bought a car already but thank you."
"No, it's me, Mr. Kosher Kondom."
I stood up, signaled to my girlfriend, and walked outside.
"Oh, sorry I couldn't hear. I was in a noisy restaurant."
"This is my new phone number. What's going on? When am I going to see you?"
"I'm dating someone, but you are very tempting."
"Yeah, let me know if things change."
"I will. It was great hearing from you."

Red Flags
❖ Age.

Insights and Lessons Learned
❖ It was just pure fun sex.
❖ It was a pleasurable and gratifying experience.
❖ He was respectful and kind to me.
❖ He elevated my self-esteem.
❖ He heightened my sensuality and sexuality like never before.
❖ He made me feel beautiful and sexy.
❖ He was appreciative that I listened to him, complimented him, and boosted his self-esteem.

❖ It can be one of the greatest experiences of your life if you have the fearlessness to be with a boy toy.

❖ Boy toys have no baggage and nothing to prove like older guys, most who had baggage and were always trying to impress me. Very refreshing to be with a boy toy.

❖ Take it for what it is. No matter how good it is, it's going to end. There's no future with a boy toy. We had little in common and we were in different stages of life.

7

AM I READY TO BE IN A RELATIONSHIP?

It was August. I was still relishing in my trysts with Mr. Kosher Kondom. We were enjoying each other and having a lot of fun. I needed and welcomed this experience in order to grow and learn and to become the sexual being that was in me all along. I knew our trysts would end at some point, but I wasn't ready for them to end just yet.

My self-esteem was soaring. My ego, well, I thought I was hot shit. Wouldn't you feel amazing if a bunch of young guys were pursuing you? I felt empowered, and in control. I was taking full advantage of my summer and feeling gratified.

I knew my worth, what I wanted, and what I deserved. But I was still in my "No Emotional Attachment" stage. The question was, could I move forward and open myself up again? Was I now ready to be in a relationship?

August

Mr. Colombian Spice: *He's Rushing in Too Fast*

I was in the midst of my summer fun. I was definitely in a phase and needed to play it out. Then Mr. Colombian Spice messaged me asking for my private email. I didn't know what to make of Mr. Colombian Spice's pics. In one pic, he seemed attractive, the other he didn't.

Mr. Colombian Spice and I emailed back and forth much more than I was accustomed to. He seemed cautious and wanted to know more about me before we talked on the phone. I went along with him. I was still curious about him.

He sent a message—
As a man who appreciates class, sophistication and, of course beauty, inside and out, I'm curious about your spiritual side. Would you like to talk to me?

Me—
Hi, I'd be happy to talk. I've become spiritual in the past couple years and go to yoga often. I strive to be positive and enjoy life. Have a good day.

Him—
I also practice yoga and go to the gym almost every day. I wake up every morning with a positive attitude. I appreciate nature and life to the fullest, I'm very respectful of other human beings, and I raised my daughters to follow as well. I also think I have the ability to rule out bad energy, and I think

your also very good natured and beautiful on the inside (where it counts the most). Have a nice day.

An hour later—

"I really like what you have conveyed in your emails to me. I would like to take you out on a date Saturday night." Mr. Colombian Spice said.

"I have another date already set up for Saturday night."

"Why don't you cancel your date and go out with me. I won't disappoint."

"I'll have to think about it. I feel that it's inconsiderate to cancel a date last minute."

I had a date with another young guy. Meaningless, really.

"I understand how you feel, but I know we're going to hit it off based on our emails and commonalities."

He spent the next hour persuading me to cancel my date. I was playing hard-to-get, of course. He owned a spice company in Colombia and traveled a lot for business. He had twin teenage girls, one who had "issues." He didn't elaborate. His ex-wife lived close by to make it easier for shared custody. He was articulate, he had a sexy Colombian accent, and I suspected he liked the finer things in life.

"Do you know where the Aventura Mall is? I live a couple minutes from there."

"Yes, I've been to Aventura Mall a couple of times."

I felt my face flush. I pass it every time I go to have sex with Mr. Kosher Kondom at his penthouse condo on the beach, down the street.

"So, will you cancel your date and meet me Saturday night?"

"Sure, you talked me into it."

"Great, you won't regret this. We will have a wonderful time; I can feel it."

"I'm looking forward to it."

I was still skeptical. Even after having a good conversation on the phone, I knew all too well we had to meet in person to feel chemistry.

That night I didn't sleep well. The anticipation kept me up for hours. Was he attractive, or just average? I was torn. He seemed serious about wanting to be in a relationship. I didn't know what I was ready for at that point.

I put on a new, brown, stretchy, clingy dress, which had a leather flowered cutout pattern piece attached to the neckline. My spikey high heels had brown and colored stripes, to coordinate with the dress. I made sure my outfit, my hair and make-up, were impeccable.

I stood in the lobby at Abe and Louie's in Boca and watched outside in anticipation for him to arrive. I was nervous, which was unlike me. I saw him arrive in his Mercedes E-class. He walked in.

"Hello." He smiled.

"Hi."

Whoa! He was so much better looking in person. Those blueish green eyes. *Wow!* A warm sensation came over me. He was finely dressed, as I predicted. He had on a simple patterned button-down long-sleeve designer shirt, jeans, and a jacket. A more conservative look.

"Let's get a drink before dinner." He suggested.

We sat at a high-top table in the bar area by the

window. He did most of the talking. I stared into his gorgeous aqua eyes as I listened and nodded. I couldn't get a read on him yet. I sipped my martini very slowly. I wanted to keep my air of sophistication in check. I could get very silly after a few sips of a drink . . . and loud.

The hostess arrived a little while later.

"Mr. Colombian Spice, we have your table waiting. Would you like to sit now?"

"Sure. Do you have one of those cozy booths for us?" He smiled at her.

"One moment. Let me check."

"This way we can sit next to each other."

We sat down in the C-shaped booth. He seemed more relaxed after his drink. We were having a great time. Time passed quickly. It was getting late. I looked around. We were the last ones sitting in the restaurant.

"Let's go somewhere else, I'm not ready for our evening to end so soon."

He gave me a kiss on the lips, which was a pleasant surprise. I had no inclination that he even liked me.

"That would be great, either am I."

He paid the valet and got the keys for both cars.

"Where should we go?"

"Mizner Park is ten minutes away. There are restaurants with bars there."

He found a parking spot and parallel parked his car. He had that I-want-to-kiss-you look on his face. After dating so much that year, I could always tell when a guy wanted to kiss me. He leaned over and started kissing me. *Hello to you too!* Deeper. *More! Please!* He read my mind. He was a damn good, passionate kisser. One of the best I'd kissed.

"Let's go for that drink, it's getting too hot in this car." He smirked at me.

"Yeah, we'd better get out of here. It's too good. You with those pretty aqua eyes staring back at me is dangerous."

We walked arm-in-arm across the courtyard.

"Why don't you take your jacket off? It's so hot out here."

He took his jacket off and began rolling up his sleeves. He gave me a sexy look, strutting his stuff. He was slim, not muscular, but in good shape. We continued to flirt with each other, laughed and had a lot of fun. Our chemistry was intense. He kept making references to how sexy Latins are.

"I love the way you dress, and I love your hair."

He stroked up and down my long brown, highlighted hair. I felt relieved that he appreciated my look after putting in such effort to look my best.

"Why thank you for the compliment. I like your look also, especially since you took off that jacket and rolled up your sleeves. You seem much more relaxed now."

It was 2:00 a.m. He drove back to the restaurant. We were in full make out mode. It lasted a long time. Finally, he walked me to my car and opened the door.

"Come to my place." He requested.

"I'm not sure that's something I'm ready to do so quickly."

Seriously? Did I just say that? Since when? Since I wanted to leave a good impression with this guy. Plus, I wasn't accustomed to screwing two different guys at the same time. That wasn't the way I rolled.

"I won't disappoint."

"Oh, I can see that! And I really want to but it's too soon. We just met."

We both got to the red light at the main road. He

opened his window and gestured to me. I opened my window.

"Come to my house." He said again.

"It's way too late. Besides, you live 45 minutes from here and you have to get up at 6:00 a.m. to go to Chicago. Three hours won't be enough time." I smirked.

I drove off. The phone rang.

"Come meet me in Chicago."

"You are tempting me."

We talked the whole way home.

Mr. Colombian Spice texted me the next day, teasing me to come to Chicago. He wouldn't be home for another week. I was tempted. The next week after that, he was taking his twins to New York City for the week. He called and asked me to go with him to Colombia on business to his spice company after his trip to NYC with his twins.

"You are really enticing me, and I love to travel. It's a passion of mine. I won't see you for a couple of weeks. I'll miss you."

I knew he was moving too fast, but we were infatuated with each other. Those feelings were affecting both of us.

He called me the next day and we shot the shit for a while. I was on a high! I let him do most of the talking, which worked well for me.

"Under no uncertain terms are you to go to Colombia. You've been on one date with him. You know nothing about him. It seems to me like he's rushing in." My therapist advised me.

"Yeah, I knew that before you said it, but we're infatuated with each other. The chemistry was hot!"

He kept in touch the entire week while in New York City. He sent pics with him and each twin. I was excited, but I kept up my trysts with Mr. Kosher Kondom. I didn't know when I would see him, or if he was going to ask me out again.

Two weeks passed—

Finally, he was back in town, and he asked me out for a drink date. I felt excited to see him again.

It was 8:00pm. We sat at the bar at J. Alexanders.
"I'm stressed. One of my twins had a meltdown earlier today."
Mr. Colombian Spice looked worn out.
"I'm so sorry to hear. Is she okay now?"
"Yes, she's better."
"Well, I hit the edge of a curb today and had a blow-out. My ex is going to be pissed because he just put four new tires on my car a month ago."
"Crazy day for both of us!"
"You could say that. Can I tell you something?" I half-smiled at him.
"Yes."
"The reason I was apprehensive to go out with you originally was because in some of your pictures you are smiling and in others you aren't. In the pics you sent me from NYC, you look happy with one twin, and stressed with the other. I couldn't get a read on you at first until I met you, and then I was very excited."
"Oh, I've never noticed that before."

We finally got into the groove where we left off a couple weeks back. Laughing, and having fun, but, not as much fun. The stress was dragging us down.

He walked me to my car. He pulled me in close. We made out. Our great kissing came back right where we left off. Our chemistry was hot. I wanted him.

"You know, you can be a lot of trouble for me." He said, in his sexy way.

"I'm sure I can."

I leaned on him. His back against the car. We continued our make out session. I wanted him right at that moment. We came up for air. I touched his face.

"Well, we'd better get going. It's been a long day for both of us."

He opened my car door and we said, "good night."

The next day—

He texted me—
Someone gave me a sore throat. I wonder who that could be?

Did he really just ask that?

Me—
I'm so sorry. Thought it was allergies, or stress.

I never heard from him again. I was upset that he would blame me for a minor scratchy throat. I didn't think it was contagious. Maybe he was upset with me for noticing his change of expression in his pictures with his twins? I would never know since he ghosted me.

I never had closure with Mr. Colombian Spice. To this day, I always wondered what could have been, but looking back, there were things that probably could have stood in the way of a long-term relationship. At that point, I knew I wasn't ready to rush to be in any relationship yet. My attitude was all about having fun. I still needed more time to evolve and grow. I couldn't decide about the kid issues, or his busy schedule. I didn't have enough information to go on.

Red Flags

- ❖ He was rushing in too fast. He asked if I was ready to be in a relationship on our first phone call before we met in person. Then he rushed in and wanted to sleep with me. He also asked me to go away with him way too soon.
- ❖ Our timing was off.
- ❖ Why did I feel the need to look perfect?
- ❖ He blamed me for giving him a sore throat.
- ❖ He had a busy schedule and traveled a lot for work.
- ❖ His daughter had issues.

Insights and Lessons Learned

- ❖ Don't rush into anything unless you are ready. I could have dropped Mr. Kosher Kondom; but driving 45 minutes at 2:00am to Mr. Colombian Spice's home, and sleeping with him, was not a rationalization in my mind. If he liked me enough, and respected me, there was no reason to rush or push to have sex with me.
- ❖ I wasn't ready to be in a relationship at that point.
- ❖ Never try to look perfect, nobody's perfect.
- ❖ Why did he blame me? I had no idea.

❖ You can decide if you want to date a guy who travels a lot for work and is very busy. It wasn't my first choice.

❖ I didn't know enough about his daughter's issues to decide if that would have been a deal breaker.

August

Triplets Guy: *The Newly Separated Guy*

Triplets Guy called on the phone as I was going to meet my friend Karen for a drink.

"Let's meet at Sushi Simon in Boynton Beach. My brother told me the sushi is great."

"Sounds good, I love sushi."

I thought about cancelling my upcoming date with him, but I'd already committed. His physique was broader than my usual type. I decided to give him a chance since he seemed upbeat and had a good personality on the phone.

I walked in. The restaurant was packed, every table full. I didn't see him. He stood up and waved from the far back.

He was much cuter and thinner in person. He was not in shape, but not as heavy as in his pics. I was pleased.

"I was looking at the menu while I was waiting for you. They have this sake sampler. Are you in?"

"Sure, that sounds good. Just to let you know, I'm a lightweight."

"It's only 5 shots, we can share."

"I think I can handle that." I tilted my head.

The waitress put down the sake sampler.

"This one is cold, this is warm, this is milky . . ."

"Do you mind if I order for both of us? My brother suggested some great rolls."

"No, I don't mind. I eat everything except for raw onions and scallions."

"Ok. No problem, we'll omit the scallions in this roll."

He picked up one of the shot glasses.

"Let's try this one now."

"You know, your cheeks are getting rosier." I said to him.

"Yeah, that happens to me. It's probably from this sake."

The waitress set down the sushi. We started to eat.

"I broke up with my wife two months ago."

"Only two months ago?"

"Yes. I think she was cheating on me. She became a party girl, got tattoos, was drinking, smoking, and staying out all night. She left me with our triplets all the time."

Triplets? No wonder she was partying all night. LOL!

"Oh, I'm so sorry to hear, that sucks. How old are your triplets?"

"They're in high school."

"That must be a challenge."

"More challenging now with the breakup."

"I feel for you. It can't be easy."

"It isn't."

I had empathy for what he was going through.

"By the way, this is some of the best sushi I've ever eaten. Tell your brother he has great taste. I'm coming back here." I smiled.

"Thank you, I will."

We left the restaurant and strolled toward my car. He put his arm around my waist. I reciprocated.

"Is this where we have the end of the night proverbial kiss." He teased.

I leaned back on my car. I started laughing, I couldn't contain myself.

"Well, I feel a little awkward since this is my first date in 18 years."

"Really? I didn't know I was your first. LOL."

"Yup."

He put his hands on my upper arms, bent forward and kissed me. He relaxed and came closer. He kissed me again. I put my hand around the back of his head and gave him more.

"You're a great kisser. It's been so long for me, I barely remember."

"Yeah, I remember my first kiss after 25 years. It was a good feeling; it comes right back to you." I smiled at him.

Don't I know it! How many guys have I kissed this year? Most of them!

We said our goodbyes.

A little while later—

I texted Triplets Guy—
Thank you very much for dinner. I enjoyed our date.

He texted back—
Our date was the best date I've been on in 18 yrs.
Would you like to go out with me Thursday?

Me—
I would love to.

He called me a few days later to confirm our date and we talked for a while. His triplets were going to a new school. He had them for two weeks. I could feel how drained he was.

We met at a local restaurant. It was an older crowd with live music. We were watching the people dancing and enjoying themselves. He just sat there and didn't say much. He seemed down and wasn't like the upbeat person I'd met. I could tell something was bothering him. He kept on bringing up his wife and how upset he was.

"Are you okay? You don't seem like the jovial guy I met."

"I'm very upset about my boy. He's having a very hard time with this. So am I."

"And the girls?"

"Not as bad. They have each other."

"Yeah, I was where you are almost a year ago. It will take some time to get through this crap. It's a process, but it does get better. I can tell you that." I put my hand on his and gave a squeeze.

He lightened up and tried to enjoy his time with me. I didn't take it personally.

"What are you doing on Saturday. I'd like to take you to the beach."

"Sure, the beach sounds good." I smiled back.

"We can have a relaxing time there."

A couple of days later, we strolled down the beach toward the water and set up the blanket. He sat there looking at the ocean not saying much. There wasn't much I could say to make him feel better.

"Would you date me if I was heavier? I just lost 20 pounds from this stress."

"Honestly, probably not. I don't usually date guys who are overweight, it's just not my thing. I'm so sorry for saying."

He looked at me with a peculiar look. He was clearly depressed and maybe a bit annoyed at my comment. He was in a bad place.

Was that shallow and tactless? I was just being honest. We all have our preferences, don't we? I pride myself on staying in shape.

"Yeah, I must admit, I don't know what to do with myself these days. I think I need time."

"Yup, I agree. Time is the only answer at this point."

We never went out again. He wasn't in an emotional state to be dating. He was in his early stage of grief. He needed time to go through the process.

Red Flags
- ❖ The newly separated guy.
- ❖ His sadness seemed to show signs of depression.
- ❖ Attachment issues.
- ❖ He was having difficulty taking care of his triplets.
- ❖ No physical or sexual chemistry. His body type didn't turn me on.

Insights and Lessons Learned
- ❖ Don't date the newly separated guy. It was too soon for him to be dating.
- ❖ Be cognizant of sadness and depression.
- ❖ His attachment issues to his wife prevented him from moving forward.
- ❖ It's up to you, but it wasn't my first choice to get involved with a guy who had to take care of triplets on his own.
- ❖ If there's no physical or sexual chemistry, move on.
- ❖ He reminded me of where I was one year ago. I was happy to be getting past most of it and had compassion for what he was going through.

September

The Equestrian Guy: *The Suspicious Older Guy*

It was clear from his pic on his horse, he had been a great looking guy when he was younger. He was still very attractive for 57. That is, if he posted his real age.

There was something about The Equestrian Guy. He seemed to ooze passion. I had a deep desire to meet him, even though I typically didn't date older guys, especially after my summer of fun with boy toys.

My trysts with Mr. Kosher Kondom had fizzled. Since I had no closure from Mr. Colombian Spice, I started questioning what I was doing. Was it time to reassess?

As we talked on the phone, he became apprehensive about meeting me. Then, he began asking many questions and didn't think the timing was right. He continued asking questions probing into my life. After several phone conversations, he realized I was unsettled, but with a lot of hesitation he set up a date to meet anyway.

I entered Abe and Louie's in Boca and walked past the lobby but didn't see him. When I got to the bar area, he was walking from the back of the restaurant toward me. As we met, he stood looking at me and smiled. He stared at me more. He put his hands on my upper arms.

"You're so cute." He smiled.

"Thank you."

We took seats at the bar, ordered drinks, and began chatting.

"You look so young and you're very pretty." He complimented.

"Thank you for saying."

There was definite chemistry between the two of us. After a short while he suggested we get dinner.

"I don't want to obligate you to take me to dinner. We were just meeting for a drink."

"Come on, let's have dinner."

We were seated in a sexy, C-shaped booth, same as with Mr. Colombian Spice. We kept the conversation light, talking about working out and staying in shape.

"Feel these abs, they're rock hard," touching his stomach.

He took my hand and put it on his abs. He was glowing.

"Wow. Those are some rock-hard abs. I'm very impressed."

"When are you getting divorced," he asked.

"I signed the papers last week."

"Oh, so you are divorced then?"

"Yes. We've been living separately for almost a year."

He started giving me advice. He had been divorced for many years. We continued chatting about all sorts of subjects, we had a lot in common.

As we were ready to exit the restaurant, he leaned toward me and gave me a brief kiss. That caught me off guard. Totally unexpected.

"Would you like to sit in my car?" He asked.

"Okay."

We left the restaurant and into his car. He leaned toward me and began kissing me. Then deeper. *Whoa . . . whoa . . . whoa!* He was the best, most passionate kisser I had ever kissed. I felt like I was melting into him. I'd never felt that "melting" feeling when I kissed a guy before. As you know, I'd kissed lots of guys by that time.

Our make out session lasted a long time, both of us not wanting it to end. It was late. He asked me out for the next day. I told him I would get back to him once I knew the time my daughter was leaving to go to her dad's. We said our goodbyes.

An hour later—

Him—
Did you get home safely?

Me—
Yes. Thank you very much for dinner, I had a great time.

The next day, I didn't hear from him, so I decided to send him a text.

Me—

I'm free to meet you this afternoon.

Him—

Thanks for letting me know, but I can't meet you today.

Where did that come from? I knew something was off. I needed clarity and closure, unlike Mr. Colombian Spice.

Me—

I don't understand. Did you misunderstand me?

Him—

Misunderstood what? I obviously had a pleasant time. I am feeling uncomfortable in that you did originally tell me that you were divorced and with papers signed; for this I very good memory. Thus, when such happens one wonders about other/future statements. Right? You have a great personality, but I think the stage that you are in and thus what you are still going through would be challenging, including distance. I suspect that there remains some grieving to get through which takes time.

Me—

I am so sorry you feel this way. I'm not deceptive, nor do I lie. We signed our divorce papers, I'm divorced. If you have concerns, I welcome any questions. As for the rest, distance can be overcome. As for grieving everyone goes through his, or her, own process. Normally, I would never respond to a text like this, I would just let it go, but we both know there was something strong between us, and I know I want to explore where it can go and think u do too. I wish you happiness and all that you wish for.

Two days later—

Him—
I hope you have a great day.

Me—
I'm happy to hear from you. I'm in NYC with my girlfriend for a few days. Have a great day.

Him—
I forgot you were going to NYC. I hope you have a great time.

Me—
Thanks

I never heard from him again.

Red Flags
- ❖ Suspicious. He didn't believe that I was divorced.
- ❖ We were in different stages of our lives.

Insights and Lessons Learned
- ❖ Communication and trust are key! Maybe he needed to see my divorce papers to believe me.
- ❖ Timing Is Everything. He sensed I was in some turmoil and knew I wasn't ready to be in a relationship at that point.

8

WHAT'S UP WITH THE NICE GUYS?

I was meeting nice guys who wanted to be in relationships. I surmised Mr. Colombian Spice and The Equestrian Guy knew I wasn't ready. I felt chemistry with both, and we had a lot in common. There were red flags, but no real deal breakers. It was time to rethink what I was doing and change my attitude.

My self-esteem was soaring. I had evolved to a place of peace in my life, and I was happy. Time to end my "No Emotional Attachment" stage. No more dating like a man. No more pursuing guys. No more boy toys.

Now was the time to open myself up again. What was my original mission? Date with intention. Persevere. Find my person.

September

The Marketing Guy: *The Nice Guy Was Afraid of Losing Her*

We were having a drink at the bar at Seasons 52 in Boca when the woman sitting next to us said, "you two make a nice couple."

"We're on our first date, we just met." I answered enthusiastically.

She looked surprised. That's because I was being flirty and trying to prod The Marketing Guy to pick up the pace as we chatted. He was polite and spoke with a slow, methodical inflection. I was trying hard to make a go of it with him. He seemed grounded and very nice so far, but I wasn't feeling any chemistry.

We were seated at a table for two and continued getting to know each other.

"I'm a widower. My wife died of cancer soon after our son was born. My parents and in-laws helped bring him up. He's a great kid."

"Wow, I commend you for that. I can't imagine how hard that was."

"It wasn't easy."

"I'm sure. I gather you had no time for a relationship in the past several years?"

"Not really. I've been getting out there for a while, but I haven't found anyone yet. I'm also busy with my career. I'm in Marketing."

"Sounds like your time is limited."

"You could say that. I have every Saturday and once during the week here and there."

He wasn't gelling with my quick wit or personality. I knew I'd be racing my car on the racetrack, while he sat in the pace car driving the first lap at 30 miles per hour.

At the end of the date, he walked me to my car.

"Can I come sit inside?"

"Okay."

"Can I kiss you?" He asked very politely.

"Yes."

A guy should never ask a woman if he can kiss her. He should just go for it! Although, I did appreciate his respectfulness.

He leaned in. He started kissing me. The kiss fell flat for me, particularly after the way The Equestrian Guy had kissed me. That was something special. It was still fresh in my mind. I wished the kiss with The Marketing Guy felt different. I felt a bit disappointed.

The next day the phone rang.

"We had a nice time last night. I'd like to take you out again." The Marketing Guy said.

"Any chance we can we be friends?"

"I guess so, but why?"

"I'm just not ready to be in a relationship yet."

I fibbed. I felt bad. I was ready to meet the guy for me, but unfortunately it wasn't him.

"I understand. I've gone out with divorcees who have gone through the process you're going through. You'll get there in time."

We became friends. He was one of the only guys I kept in touch with. We would talk on the phone from time to time. I would ask him for advice when some bullshit happened to me.

Months later I asked The Marketing Guy a question about relationships.

"I thought you weren't ready to be in a relationship yet. I was hoping when you were ready, you'd come back to me."

"I'm not in a relationship. We've only been on a few dates. I'm not sure if it'll go anywhere. I like him, and we have great chemistry."

We would meet up once in a while for a bite to eat and talk on the phone from time to time.

Months later he invited me to his 50th birthday party. Soon after he moved out of state to take a new job. A year or so later he was in town visiting. We met for dinner.

"After all this time you still haven't found anyone. Why do you think that is other than the fact you work a lot and take care of your son? But he's almost grown up." I asked.

"Well, the pool of Jewish women where I live now is sparse. It's hard to find someone to have a relationship with."

"Yeah, that's tough, if you want to date in the same religion. But nobody?"

"I keep meeting these separated or newly divorced women that I end up giving advice to. I wind up holding their hands, while I listen to their woes. They have a lot of baggage."

"Maybe you need to start meeting women who have less baggage. You aren't their therapist."

"Honestly, I'm afraid of someone dying on me. I don't think I can bare that again." He said with a sad look on his face.

"Wow, I have no words. I feel for you."

My empathy was overflowing. That brought it all to the surface for me. He carried all that baggage for all these years and couldn't let go of his fear. I felt sorry for him.

We stayed in touch every now and again.

A couple of years later—

We hadn't been in touch for a while. Then, we met up again.

"What's going on with dating now that you moved back in town." I asked him.

"Every time I meet someone and tell them I travel a lot for work their eyes get glossed over. Now, I've decided to move again, close to Port Saint Lucie. There are more gun ranges there, and shooting is a hobby of mine. I might be boring, but I am a nice guy."

"Yes, you are one of the nicest guys I've ever met." I smiled.

I was saddened that he hadn't met his person.

Red Flags
- ❖ I felt no chemistry.
- ❖ Our personalities didn't mesh, and we didn't have much in common.
- ❖ He had limited time to date.
- ❖ He was afraid of someone dying on him again.
- ❖ He hadn't been in a long-term relationship in years.

Insights and Lessons Learned
- ❖ Chemistry is too important to ignore.

- ❖ We were not a match.
- ❖ My choice was to date a guy who had time for me.
- ❖ I had empathy for him. He was deserving of love.
- ❖ I hoped he could get past his fear of someone dying on him and meet his person.

September

Mr. Don't Suck Me: *The Nice Guy Had Hang-Ups*

I walked into J. Alexander's in Boca and saw Mr. Don't Suck Me straddling a bar stool with a glass of wine in hand. He was much balder than I expected, but he was fairly attractive. His profile pics were dated. In his pics he had a head of light brown hair that was thin and receding.

"I'm a condo lawyer. I live on the west coast of Florida. I come every week to see my young son."

Lawyer? West coast? Young son? Red flags.

He had a good personality, and we laughed a lot. I really enjoyed my time with him. He seemed like a well-balanced guy.

"I must tell you something. I had a soccer accident when I was a boy. They didn't fix my leg properly."

He demonstrated by walking in a circle with a noticeable limp. I was more concerned about him living far away from me and having a young son than his gait.

As we walked out of J's, I watched as he teeter-tottered with every step. Teeter-tottered. Teeter-tottered. I was caught off guard, but I tried not to let it fluster me. We stood by my car.

"I had a great time tonight." He said to me.

"Me too. You made me laugh a lot."

He leaned in for a kiss, lightly brushing my lips, but didn't touch me. He kept his hands by his side, giving me a single kiss, with a closed mouth, again. He skimmed my lips once more. I moved closer to him and put my hand around his head. I wanted a little more. He kissed me again, mouth shut. Still not touching me. I drew his bottom lip in very softly.

"What are you doing?" He said in a shocked tone.

He pulled away abruptly and backed up.

"I wasn't doing anything, why?"

Uh oh? I looked at him inquisitively.

"Well, we just met."

Oh, no! This isn't good! Wasn't that something I was supposed to say? I felt a shift and the need to go. He still had that look like I did something freaky to him.

"I have to leave now." I opened my car door.

Run—Run! No worries, he can't catch you. Oops, that wasn't a nice thing to think.

"Take care." I said, as I got into my car.

I was gentle. I didn't bite. It was the complete opposite of when The Vampire clamped down so hard on my neck that he left bite marks on me. I didn't know what to make of the reaction I got from Mr. Don't Suck Me. It was very off-putting. He made me feel bad. It hit a trigger, which came too close to home. I had to remember it was his hang-up, not mine. I would have to let that go.

He texted and asked me out again. I thanked him and told him we were not a match.

Red Flags

❖ He had hang-ups. His reaction made me feel bad.

❖ He lived too far away.
❖ He had a young son.

Insights and Lessons Learned
❖ Don't allow anyone to make you feel bad. It was his hang-up, not mine.
❖ Dating someone who lived hours away wasn't my first choice.
❖ Don't date a guy with a young child if it doesn't work for you.

September-October

Construction Guy: *The Nice Guy Didn't Know How to Pursue and Was Self-Conscious About His Body*

We met at The Office on the Ave in Delray for lunch. Construction Guy had a cute face and great smile.

"I've never been to Atlantic Avenue. I figured I would meet you here since you live closer, and I was on a job nearby. I live in Deerfield and am busy with my twin boys."

"The Ave is great. It's always busy and lively here. Lots of restaurants, bars, and shops. It's a great place to hang out. How old are your boys?"

"They're teenagers. I have sole custody. Their mother wasn't fit to take care of them."

"Wow, sorry to hear."

"I'm not. I spend a lot of time with them. Sometimes she takes them when it's convenient for her."

"Well, at least she does spend some time with them."

"Yes, when she feels like it. I work in construction. I used to own my own company, but it went under."

"Whoa, that sucks. Sorry to hear."

He told me what happened to the failed business, then talked more about his job in construction, and his sons.

"I have to get going. I only get an hour for lunch. How about we get together this Friday night? My twins will be at their friend's house. Why don't you come to Deerfield, and we can walk to a restaurant near the beach?"

"Sure, that sounds good." I smiled.

"I'll text you the time and my address."

"Great."

He was very upbeat and cordial. He had cute dimples in his cheeks. He was heavier than his pics, but he seemed like a genuine guy, so I decided to see him again.

I arrived at his house.

"Hi, come on in."

"Thanks."

"It's a very small house, not much to see. I moved after the business went under."

"We all do what we have to, right?"

"Yes."

"Do you wear contacts? You have beautiful, blue eyes. Has anyone ever told you that?" He asked.

"Yes. Thanks. No contacts. These are my real eyes. I get that compliment a lot."

We were sitting on his couch talking when he came in for a kiss. He started to kiss me deeper. Then deeper. We came up for air.

"I bet you didn't expect me to kiss you like that, did you?" A hint of pride in his voice.

"Nope. It was way sooner than expected, but I appreciate your spontaneity."

"Well, I wanted to kiss you after lunch, but it was our first date, and we were standing on Atlantic Avenue. My friend gave me advice after I told him I liked you. I haven't been in a relationship in years. I've been busy with my twins."

He was a helicopter dad. He was so busy all these years with his twins, he didn't make time to date, and had no idea how to pursue me. I tried prompting him, but I stopped because I didn't have the desire to chase after him and make dates. He needed to figure it out on his own.

We dated for six weeks. We liked each other, but I didn't feel any physical or sexual chemistry toward him. It just wasn't there. He was overweight and self-conscious about his belly, and the shape of his schlong. That gave me pause. I was surprised he divulged that information.

My cousin came down from New York to visit and asked me to go on a cruise with her. When I got back four days later, he accused me of cheating on him while on the cruise. It wasn't true, but it didn't matter. I knew this guy wasn't for me. We had nothing in common, and we were not a match.

Red Flags
- ❖ He hadn't been in a relationship in years, and he couldn't figure out how to pursue me and make time to date.
- ❖ No physical or sexual chemistry.

* His self-consciousness about his body, and other insecurities were a turn-off.
* We had nothing in common.

Insights and Lessons Learned

* Don't pursue any guy. If he can't figure out how to pursue you and make the time for you, move on.
* Once again, you can't create physical or sexual chemistry.
* If a guy is uncomfortable in his own skin, and it's a turn-off, don't waste time.
* We weren't a match for many reasons.

October

Mr. Pecker: *The Nice Conservative Genteel Guy Was Rigid and Inexperienced*

"We've been watching each other for weeks. Would you like to go out this weekend?" Mr. Pecker asked me.

I didn't remember seeing Mr. Pecker online before. He seemed like a refined guy. He had professional pics on his profile, and one, he was posing like a fitness model. His body was small muscled and ripped to shreds. That turned me on.

"Let's meet on Atlantic Avenue at the bar for drinks." Mr. Pecker said.

"Great, looking forward to meeting you."

As I exited the bathroom of the restaurant, I recognized Mr. Pecker walking toward me.

"Hi." I smiled at him.

"Oh, hi. How about we have dinner inside the restaurant instead of drinks? It's quite noisy and dark in this bar."

"That would be great."

He was impeccably dressed. He had on slacks, a button-down, and sport jacket; a bit conservatively dressed for me. He had grayish blond hair, a small turned up nose, and very fair skin. Attractive, however, not my usual type. I like dark haired guys.

"I eat a very strict diet, only protein, no carbohydrates, and I only eat dessert on my birthday. I treat myself to fruit." Mr. Pecker was glancing at the menu.

"Wow. You're very disciplined. I eat everything in moderation. I try not to restrict anything, but I do try to eat on the cleaner side."

Fruit isn't a real dessert. I guess we won't be having a Cannoli, an ice cream sundae, or a chocolate molten lava cake tonight. Now that's what I call dessert!

"I have a trainer at the gym. I go every morning at 4:00am. I'm trying out for a movie tomorrow. I'm an aspiring actor and model."

Model—Actor? A late start for a 56-year-old, but I guess it's never too late.

"That's fabulous, I hope you get the part. I go to the gym and do yoga on a regular basis. I've worked out my whole life."

"You have beautiful hair." He spoke softly and had a calm disposition.

"Thank you."

"One time this woman came to our date with a wig on."

"What? Are you kidding me?" I rolled my eyes.

"She said she didn't have time to wash her hair."

"Ooh. That's Gross."

"I didn't like that at all. I'm very clean. I clean my house before the cleaning woman comes."

"Yes, cleanliness is important to me. My house is always clean and in order."

We had good conversation about a lot of interesting topics. The conversation flowed really well. It was a pleasurable night. He paid the bill.

"Did you valet your car?" He asked.

"Yes, I always valet at night. I want to stay safe."

He walked with me to the valet and paid my bill.

"Do you mind driving me to my car? I parked down the street in the bank parking lot."

"Sure."

We drove a couple blocks, next to Vic & Angelo's.

"Right there." He pointed.

He leaned in for a kiss. He pulled away. Then, Peck—Peck. He was very gentle. Lips closed. Peck—Peck. I parted my lips. He wasn't getting it. Peck— Peck. I tried again to kiss him, lips parted, softly. Peck—Peck. I tried to coax him to stop pecking and really kiss me, but I was unsuccessful. There was no way I was going to suck in his bottom lip like I did with Mr. Don't Suck Me. You know how he made me feel.

"You're a great kisser." He said to me.

"Thank you."

I'm a great kisser? That wasn't kissing. Those were only slow, exaggerated kisses. Just wait until I really kiss him! We said our good-byes.

I called my girlfriend Melissa who had dated Mr. All-Around-Town. She'd been on dating sites for years, and was a pro. She always gave great advice.

"What do you suggest I do? He pecked at me very tentatively with his mouth closed. Then, he told me I was a great kisser. I really like him, but I don't want to scare him off. He seems inexperienced."

"Well, I would feel him out, and when you're ready, you should ask him to give you his tongue when he kisses you. You can teach him how."

"Who wants to teach a 56-year-old how to kiss? He happens to be one of the most upstanding guys I've ever met. Not much of a personality yet but kind."

"Just try it and see if he's receptive."

"Ok, thanks for the advice. I'm going to give it a try . . . maybe."

A week later—

I wanted to go into this second date with no expectations, but I was actually excited for a change. Although, I was a little apprehensive about the kissing situation.

I picked out a see-through, V-neck, floral-patterned, lavender top with a ruffle around the back of the neck and put a camisole underneath it. I paired it with eggplant-colored jeans. I got the sense he was very traditional. The top would have been too sexy with just a bra underneath.

There was a tropical depression in South Florida. As I entered Houston's in Boca, I saw Mr. Pecker at the bar, wine glass in his hand, hand in pocket, standing very stoically. I smiled. He softened his stance. He held up his glass of white wine and smiled back. He was wearing a pair of dark green slacks and a white button-down shirt. Maybe he came from work?

I was jostling my umbrella trying to close it. Water was dripping on me, and my pocketbook was falling off my shoulder. He took the umbrella. I was sliding the strap of my handbag back onto my shoulder when he handed me a small plastic container.

"Put this in your pocketbook."

I did as he asked.

"I got here early and asked for the booth in the back. It's private and quiet up there."

"That's very thoughtful of you."

We were seated in the booth.

"I got the acting part in the movie. I start tomorrow." Mr. Pecker was beaming.

"Wow, that's wonderful. Congratulations."

We held hands and flirted with each other while we waited for our dinner. Then, the power went out in the restaurant. He leaned in and gave me a peck.

"I'm glad the power is out. I loved those kisses you gave me last time."

Peck—Peck. The power came back on. The waitress arrived.

"I'm so sorry the power keeps going out, but this heavy rain isn't letting up. I hope to have your dinner soon."

"No hurry." He smiled at her.

She left.

"I like when the power goes out."

He gave me another peck. The power went out again. Peck—Peck. I wasn't ready to do the give-me-your-tongue-thing yet. We were in public. Maybe later. Peck—Peck.

I felt as if he was trying to be a bit sexy and cool, trying to be someone he really wasn't, just to impress me.

"Is having sex the norm after the third date? I'm in no way insinuating this. I want to get to know you, and it's just funny to hear people go by this silly rule."

"There are no rules Mr. Pecker. We don't need to rush in. We can do whatever is comfortable for the both of us."

"After my divorce I went out with this woman. We didn't kiss for nine months and didn't have sex until after one year."

"Oh. I give you credit, that's a long time. I don't know how you held out for so long."

"I took my profile down off all the sites. I want more than dating. I want us to be in a relationship if you are interested?"

"I'm open to it if we find that we're a good fit."

What do I do about the kissing obstacle? The tell-tale sign of a bad lover is a bad kisser! I had to decide if I would even try the give-me-your-tongue technique.

"Do you know what the dress code is for our third date?" He asked.

"No." I gave his hand a squeeze.

"I'm taking you to the beach on Saturday, so wear your sexiest bathing suit."

"Well, I hope that our date is better than my last two beach dates."

"Oh, it will be. I'm going to take you into the ocean, and I want you to wrap your legs around me while we float around."

Did he just say that? That comment seemed as if it was out of his element. *Hmm?* He put his hand on my leg. I decided to take a chance and put my leg on top of his.

"I like that you did that. I thought you might do something like that."

"Well, I like you and I'm an affectionate person."

I put my hand on his face and gave him a couple of soft, exaggerated kisses.

"I can't get enough of your kisses."

We finished dinner.

"You go to the restroom first, then I'll go. You have the package in your purse."

I went to the restroom, looked in my bag and took out the package. *Seriously? Are you kidding me right now?* I went back to the table.

"Here you go."

I handed him the package with one throw-away toothbrush in it. He left the table and went to the restroom.

He put his arm around me as we walked to my car and pulled me in close to keep me dry. He got in the passenger seat. He leaned in. Peck—Peck. Peck—Peck. I thought he would kiss me for reals this time. Didn't we just brush our teeth?

"You make me feel young again, kissing in the car like this." He smiled.

"Glad to hear."

He has no idea how many times I've done this? Peck— Peck. I needed to step it up.

I whispered to him, "give me your tongue."

I sucked his tongue in very gently.

"Move your tongue with me." I directed him.

"Oh my, I've never kissed like that before. I like it."

Really? How could that be? I took his tongue in my mouth again and moved slowly. He was getting the hang of it. The kissing was a little better.

"I better get going. I have a very early wake up time tomorrow." He said in a subdued tone.

The next day—

> He sent a text—
> Love that whole tongue thing we had going on last night!
>
> Me—
> Me too, there's more where that came from.
>
> Him—
> Can't wait to go to the beach and go in the ocean with you. I've been fantasizing about it.
>
> Me—
> I'm very excited to go with you.

Friday, the day before our beach date—

> Him—
> I can't wait to kiss you that way again.
>
> Me—
> I can't wait to kiss you back.

Saturday, 7:30am—

> Mr. Pecker—
> I'm sorry. I can't make our beach date today.
>
> Me—
> Is everything ok?

No response—

Did he really just do that? Yup, he canceled our date, and ghosted me. I was so upset. Why did he cancel our date? Why didn't he respond to my text? Especially after he said he took his profile down off all the sites and wanted to be in a relationship. It made no sense. I liked him. I actually teared up.

After the initial shock of being blown off at 7:30 a.m., I thought about everything. His lifestyle and schedule seemed very rigid. I was a go-with-the-flow type. He ate a very strict diet. I ate on the cleaner side, everything in moderation, and I loved to eat dessert! He was a conservative Catholic. I was a non-religious Jew. He worked out with a trainer at 4:00 a.m. In no way was I getting up at 4:00 a.m. to work-out. The brush-our-teeth-after-dinner-thing felt a bit extreme to me. Particularly, because he wasn't even opening his mouth to kiss me. Since he never French kissed before, I had a sinking feeling he had very little experience in the bedroom. Maybe he was apprehensive about the third date rule and thought we had to have sex after our beach date. Who knows? I clearly wasn't the right girl for him, nor him for me. But I was still upset for several days.

The least he could've done was to answer my text. That would have been the appropriate thing to do. Specifically, because he was very proper. That really bothered me.

One month later—

Mr. Pecker—
I had a death in the family. You're a great woman. You deserve the best.

I wanted to blast his ass. But of course, I took the high road and acted like a lady. Always cordial.

Me—
So sorry to hear. Thank you for saying. I think you're a great guy. It's nice to hear from you.

That was the last message I received from him. The whole thing was very strange. I'd seen him the entire month, active on that dating site. My belief was that he was afraid of being with me and knew he might not measure up. We would not be a good fit in the long run. Maybe he did me a favor?

Red Flags

- He had never French kissed.
- He seemed inexperienced.
- He lived a very rigid lifestyle and was too conservative for me. Was he OCD?
- We had different religious beliefs.
- Our daily habits did not align. His habits were too restrictive for me.

Insights and Lessons Learned

- Moving forward, I had no intention of instructing any guy in the art of French kissing.
- Being with an experienced guy who was a great kisser and lover would be my first choice.
- Open-minded guys, not someone who was rigid, OCD, or conservative, were a better fit for me.
- Similar religious and/or spiritual beliefs were my first choice.
- I wanted a guy with similar daily habits to mine.

❖ Do compromise, don't settle. Don't try to force something that may not work. We had too many differences, we were not a match.

October-November

The Marriage Coach: *The Nice Guy Was Delusional About His Career*

I left to meet The Marriage Coach at Panera Bread for lunch in Boca on a beautiful warm fall day. I was wearing one of my short, cute dresses.

He arrived a few minutes later. I recognized him immediately. *Hello gorgeous!* He was tall and thin, and was striking, with slicked back shiny jet-black hair, piercing blue eyes, and dimples in his cheeks. He looked like he could be a model, even at 49-years-old. His profile pics were taken by a professional photographer.

"Hi." He smiled.

"Nice to meet you."

We ordered our lunch and sat down.

"I originally worked as a stock analyst on Wall Street for over ten years. I still own an 1800 square foot loft in Chelsea but haven't been there in a while."

"I love New York, it's one of my favorite places to go. I go quite often with my friend D. I grew up in New Jersey." I responded.

"Now, I'm a Marriage Coach. I love what I do."

A Marriage . . . what? Those gorgeous blue eyes!

"I've never heard of a Marriage Coach. Do you have formal training? Did you have a degree in Psychology?"

"No. I don't need a degree. I've studied the bible, psychology, men, and women, and I wrote a book about relationships. I organize and conduct three-hour seminars with couples."

He did most of the talking. He was upbeat and personable. He spoke passionately about his seminars. I wasn't sure I agreed with his philosophy, but I listened. He continued talking. I knew nothing about the bible, but I kept up with him when he talked about psychology. I'd spent lots of time at my therapist and learned a lot about myself and the different behaviors people exhibit.

What I didn't understand was, he was divorced. He had no degree, had failed relationships, and I had no idea what made him think he had the credentials for his business. I kept that to myself.

He continued to talk. I was patient to listen for a such a long time. I wanted to see if there was a lighthearted side to him. It was time to throw him off his game.

"I just missed what you said. I was so busy looking at your gorgeous blue eyes and sexy dimples, I couldn't concentrate." I tilted my head and gave him a flirty look.

He got a bit embarrassed, looked down, then giggled. Yeah, he was the typical guy who I could throw off course when I was flirty. I had his number. He was trying to impress me. How many times have these guys tried to impress me? Too many.

We were almost two hours in. He was talking about the book he wrote.

"I have to pick up my daughter from school now." I interjected.

"Come to my car. I'll give you a copy of my book. I self-published it."

"Wow, that's some book."

The big hardcover looked as if it was over 1000 pages.

"Yes, it took me a while."

"I'd say!"

"Can I kiss you? I wasn't sure because you mentioned that guy who overstepped. I didn't think you kissed on the first date."

"Of course, you can kiss me. You misunderstood when I brought up Mr. All-Around-Town. He was too aggressive and ungentlemanly, trying to stick his tongue down my throat after I asked him not to kiss me the first two times. He dated one of my best friends for a couple of months."

"Oh no, that wasn't good."

He bent down to kiss me. He kissed me a few more times, lips parted.

"You have great lips." His dimples out for display.

"You're not so bad yourself." I touched his chest, then held his hand.

"Are you free on Friday night?"

"Sure."

"I'll call in a couple of days. I have my five-year-old son this week."

"Okay, sounds great."

Five-year-old son? That's a little young. Why didn't I remember that? Maybe he hadn't told me? It didn't matter. I was mesmerized by his piercing blue eyes, and beautiful face.

A few days later—

We met at J. Alexanders in Boca and were seated in a booth. He sat next to me. He put his arm around me and gave me a kiss.

"Let's talk about our personal lives tonight, instead of business. I've been having some epiphanies this week. I'd like to tell you about them." I said, as I held his hand and looked into his piercing blue eyes.

He began talking about the events from his past few days. Then, I elaborated on my epiphanies.

"I feel empowered, and I have peace and happiness in my life. It's taken me all this year to evolve and grow."

"Wow, that's wonderful."

"Thank you. It's been a learning experience and I'm happy I had this journey." I beamed.

We finished dinner. We got in his car. He pulled me in. He started kissing me. There I was again, making out in a car. I just couldn't stop myself. I was having a lot of fun. He was a good kisser. Making out some more.

I was enjoying my time with him but began to see some signs of financial woes. He asked if I knew of any couples who would want to attend his seminar. I wouldn't go to his seminar, so why would I recommend it to any of my friends? I didn't believe he had a viable business, but it wasn't my place to say.

The next week, he suggested hanging out at my house and watching a movie. I was fine with it. It was an easy, casual night. He stayed the night. We enjoyed our time together. He was always kind and cheerful, with those dimples out on display.

He stayed in touch but didn't set up a date for the next week. Maybe he had his son that week, or maybe his money problems were his issue? He didn't say. I decided not to wait around for him. I really liked him but kept my options open and kept dating.

Mr. P90X was a divorced guy who took me on two dates. The second date, he divulged he had just gotten fired from his management position with a massage company and was starting a telemarking job, which he knew nothing about. That seemed sketchy. The P90X t-shirt he was wearing was too small and hugged his belly. It was a turn-off. Coincidentally, I happened to be dating two guys in the same situation, at the same time. Both seemed to be having money issues and their careers were in flux. I let him go.

A week later—

The Marriage Coach finally told me he was having severe money issues and had leveraged his condo in NYC. There wasn't any equity left, it was upside down, so he couldn't sell it. He had his five-year-old son the whole weekend, so he set up a date for that Sunday night. The red flags were out, but I liked him and still wanted to play it out.

"I'll pick you up at 7:00."

"Okay, see you then."

When The Marriage Coach arrived, he seemed off, and his eyes looked glassy. He gave me a big hug.

"Hi Sunshine, let's go to the movies."

"That sounds like a plan." I gave him a peck on the lips.

He handed the woman at the box office his credit card.

"Sorry, we only take cash at this discount theater."

He fished in his wallet and found some cash. We sat down. He leaned to the side and pulled me toward him. He started making out with me. He was swirling his tongue more fervently than usual. It was as if he had an urge to take me right then and there. We came up for air. Out of the corner of my eyes, I could see the old people ogling and I got a bit embarrassed.

"Is that you Valerie?" She said to me.

I turned around and saw the two older women who were receptionists at my aunt's nursing home.

"Hi, how are you."

"You two make a nice couple."

"Thanks." We both said.

Other people were gawking at us. I was surprised they didn't say . . . you two should get a room. I sank down into the seat. He took his hand from around my neck and held my hand.

After the movie ended, he said, "let's go eat, I'm starving. I haven't eaten all day."

"Why haven't you eaten anything today? It's 9:30, that's crazy."

"I'm feeling sick, I think I have a fever." I felt his head.

"Yup, your very hot."

"Do you want to call it a night and drop me off?" I said in a sympathetic tone.

"No. I'm hungry. Let's go eat."

He drove down the street.

"Fuck! That's where I lived with my ex-wife. That place was such a shithole . . . blah, blah, blah."

I was surprised and caught off guard. I'd never heard him speak in an angry tone before. He was always friendly and cheerful, always a gentleman.

We entered the restaurant and sat down.

"We'll share the chicken parm." The Marriage Coach said to the waitress.

"There's a sharing charge."

"Are you kidding me? That's ridiculous at this time of night."

"It's ok, let's order two things." I put my hand on his and gave a slight squeeze.

"No, that's stupid. I don't want to eat that much. Let's just share a pizza."

"Our pizzas are smaller individual ones. There's still a sharing charge."

He went ballistic. He started yelling loudly and angrily. I tried to calm him down, but nothing I said was getting through. I was offended. Luckily, the restaurant was empty. I wanted the night to be over.

"We'll have a pizza, and I'll have a side salad."

He didn't stop. He was irate. I'd never seen this side of him, ever. I just wanted to go home! I was so disenchanted.

The check came. He handed the waitress his credit card.

"Your credit card is declined."

He handed her another card.

"That one's declined also."

He looked in his wallet. He had four dollars. The bill was $16 dollars. I pulled out my wallet.

"Here." I handed him a twenty.

"Thank you, I'll pay you back."

He drove to my house. I was silent. It's rare when I'm silent. He parked the car.

"I guess I'm not staying the night, am I?"

"No, I don't think that's a good idea. Go home and get some rest."

"Good night, Sunshine." He smiled at me.

"Feel better. Good night."

Did that really just happen? Yup, it did.

He called me the next day and left a message, like nothing happened. No apology. No remorse. I probably should have texted, or called him back, but I didn't see the point. I ghosted him. He didn't even try to text or call me back again, even after dating for six weeks. That told me everything.

Red Flags
* He was delusional about his career. His business venture was failing.
* He was having major money issues.
* His severe money issues seemed to bring out his anger.
* He had a young child.

Insights and Lessons Learned
* My choice moving forward was to only go out with guys who had a real career, a stable job, or were retired.
* It's up to you if you want to be in a relationship with a guy who is financially unstable. Going forward, I would only go out with guys who were financially stable.
* Money issues or not, don't bother with guys who have anger issues.
* Being in a relationship with a guy who had a very young child was not my first choice.

9
NO EXPECTATIONS

After one year of dating, my expectations of meeting a great guy had diminished. The revolving door of subpar men had brought me to the point of giving up the online menagerie. I had met a few nice guys; however, I still hadn't met the guy for me.

My attitude towards dating remained indifferent. I felt empowered. I would listen to my intuition and set my boundaries. I wasn't going to settle for just anyone.

Even though I was ready to quit and get off the sites, my mission to find a great guy was still looming in my mind. I'd been on over 150 dates, dated more than 75 guys, exchanged hundreds of pseudo flirty texts, engaged in lots of small talk, and hadn't met my person. Before quitting altogether, I decided to do one last search to see if anyone different popped up. I started scrolling through the gamut of guys. The usual suspects. But wait. Who is he?

November-November

Mr. Five Love Languages: *The Guarded Guy Was Afraid of Getting Hurt Again*

I'd never seen Mr. Five Love Languages on any dating site. He looked really attractive and had the body type I liked. He was very clear in stating who he was and what he was looking for in a relationship. It was refreshing for a change. I put him in my "favorites." He messaged me and asked for my phone number. I got excited.

The phone rang a while later.

"Hi, I'm Mr. Five Love Languages. You seem like you know what you're looking for in a relationship. It's very interesting that you put it out there."

"That's funny, I thought the same about you. I definitely know what I'm looking for, especially after all the guys I've dated this past year."

"We can definitely talk more about that when we meet." He spoke in a soothing tone.

"Are you available to meet for dinner tomorrow night?"

"No, I have plans. How about lunch after my yoga class, if that works for you."

"Call me after yoga."

"Great, I'll talk to you tomorrow."

Call him? Mr. Five Love Languages seemed apathetic. What's that all about?

The next day—

I wasn't going to call Mr. Five Love Languages.

I texted him—
GM, I'm back from yoga.

"Hi, how was your yoga class?" He asked.
"Great. How are you doing today?"
"Fine. I just finished my workout. I was wondering if it would be better if we met for dinner next weekend instead of lunch today. It's nice to have drinks before dinner to loosen up."
"I'll leave that up to you."
"No, that's fine. I was thinking out loud. Let's meet at J. Alexander's in Boca at 12:30."
He didn't seem very interested in meeting me. My expectations dropped to below zero.

I threw on a pair of skinny blue jeans and a royal blue, stretchy, clingy top that coordinated with my blue eyes. I put on a pair of four-inch black wedges. I still had to look good, even though I wasn't excited to meet him.

As I strolled through the parking lot in a nonchalant, no expectations kind-of-way, with my yoga buzz on, he saw me coming his way. Our eyes met. We smiled at each other. I just stared back at him with a smirk on my face, and kept walking, actually strutting, toward him. I felt my body get excited.
"Hi!" We both said at the same time.
He had a big smile on his face. *Whoa!* That dimple in his chin! And one in his cheek too. He had that lean, smaller muscled body type that turned me on. About eight inches taller than me in my heels. *Ooh, ooh, ooh! Rein it in! Get a grip!*
We walked to J's and were seated in a booth by the window. I looked into his brown eyes through his rimless

rectangular glasses, but I couldn't take my eyes off his chin and full lips. I needed to focus.

"I have to admit, I posted my age as five years younger. I'm 51. Same as you, correct?" Mr. Five Love Languages asked.

"Yup."

"I'm having a hard time finding women my age who look younger and are in good shape. My friends and family suggested I put a younger age on my profile."

"Yeah, I get that. I've had the same issues. Darn, and I thought you were 46." I gave him a playful look.

"How do you stay in such great shape?" I asked.

His defined biceps stuck out of his short sleeve black polo shirt.

"I did gymnastics when I was a kid. Now I play tennis, mountain bike, and go to the gym. I used to be on a roller hockey team also. I've been an athlete all my life."

"What a coincidence, I competed in gymnastics when I was in high school and college. I used to roller skate when I was a kid, and because I was so little and flexible, I won the limbo contest every weekend. Now, I work out, and as you know, I do yoga on a regular basis."

"I'm curious to know if we have the same wants in a relationship. Do you like to show affection?" He asked.

"Absolutely. Somebody who isn't affectionate would be a real deal breaker for me. I lived without affection for too many years." I admitted.

"Me too. What is your feeling on chemistry?"

"Wow, you're jumping right in there with the important questions, aren't you?" I teased.

"I don't like wasting time anymore, particularly if we aren't on the same page. I've been in a few relationships since getting divorced five years ago and want to find the right person for me."

He had a soft tone and calm demeanor. It was refreshing when a man spoke his mind and knew what he wanted.

"Yeah, I agree. Chemistry is a must for me now. I tried dating all different types to see if there would be chemistry, but it didn't work for me."

And yes! I was feeling it bad for him already! Even as straight-faced as he was, asking those questions. I kept staring at his lips, that dimple in his chin, and his extremely attractive, angular face.

"You mentioned all those dates you've been on this year. What's that all about?" He probed.

"Well, I was married for 25 years. The divorce was finalized 2 months ago. I began dating and wanted to have fun and needed practice. It's been a real crapshoot."

"I'd like to hear about some."

"Some are funny, some not-so, and of course, most are enlightening, but it brought me to where I am now. I'm in a great place. I've had epiphanies and feel empowered. I needed this last year to learn about myself and grow, and I think it was a great experience for me. I just got to the point where I feel worn down being on these dating sites. I was doing one last search and just about to get off when I saw you."

"Yes, I just got back on this week. I ended a relationship a couple of months ago."

"That's not that long ago. How are you doing?"

"I'm getting past it. She was very nice, but I realized she wasn't my person."

"We sometimes realize over a period of time."

"Yes. Usually at three months we start seeing the bad come out."

"Sometimes sooner. LOL." I quipped.

"Yes. Last question. Do you like to kiss?" He asked.

"I'll let you figure that one out for yourself." I gave him my sure-you-can-kiss-me flirty look.

"Well then, that's all that's left for us to do."

He had a big fat smile on his face like when we met. It made me feel warm all over. We were ready to leave, but there was a torrential downpour.

"I'll run to my car and get my umbrella."

He gave me his hand and lifted me out of the booth.

"Be careful."

"Okay."

He held my elbow as I walked down the steps. He was protective. I liked that.

"I'll be right back."

He was stroking his rain-soaked, black, wavy hair straight back with his fingers, as he walked back into J's. He put his arm around me and pulled me in close to keep me from getting wet. He had a gentle touch. We walked to the parking lot. He guided me to the passenger door of his car. He got in the driver's side and threw the umbrella into the back seat.

He put his left hand on my face and started to kiss me. He put his right arm around my upper back. We intertwined our tongues together in a slow rhythm. We were in full embrace as he stroked the side of my face with his thumb. There was a gentleness about him. He had his own special way of kissing me with his full sexy lips. I was turned on. We came up for air.

"On your profile you said you like to drive fast cars?" He looked into my eyes.

"I love to drive fast cars. Are you surprised?"

"Yes, I am. You don't seem the type."

"My look is deceiving." I replied.

"I haven't met any women who like speed. I'm an adrenaline junkie; I love all things fast."

He began kissing me again. This guy kissed me like no other. The only guy who kissed me in a similar way was The Equestrian Guy. Most of the others were average at best or they sucked.

"I want to hear more about how your looks are deceiving."

"Oh really?" I smirked.

A little mystery was good for him. We would stop and smile at each other in silence. We looked into each other's eyes. It felt amazing and vulnerable at the same time! Our making out intensified. He was making me crazy! I wanted him badly! He held me tighter. Very passionate. It lasted for an hour . . . maybe more. We could have stayed there in the car fogging up the windows for hours, or for all night, if it was up to me. He had me by the way he held me and kissed me. He seemed as if he oozed sensuality—but not at first glance.

"Well, at least we had an excuse to stay here making out, it was raining so hard."

"Yeah, I'm glad it finally let up, and the sun is coming out. I have to go soon." I responded.

"I'll walk you to your car. I'd like to take you out next Saturday night. Maybe we can get together on Tuesday night? I'll call you."

"That sounds great. I had a great time. Thank you for lunch—and the amazing kissing."

"You are very welcome . . . it was my pleasure."

He held my face and gave me a quick kiss, then enveloped me in his arms with a very tight hug. I put my arms around him and squeezed tightly. He smelled so good. I fit into his arms and body perfectly. I felt the hard muscles in his chest. I didn't want to leave. We stood there a few more seconds in the embrace. He opened my car door, and we said goodbye. I was on a high. I couldn't wait to see him Tuesday night.

A couple of hours later, I went on my night date with The Marriage Coach. You know what happened with him. I was upset after that horrendous night. I really liked him, but his angry behavior took me by surprise. I still couldn't believe he acted that way. I would never go out with The Marriage Coach again.

Luckily for me, timing was on my side, and I met Mr. Five Love Languages, or I might've been much more upset. My mind was focused on him, for the moment.

After I got home from my date with The Marriage Coach, a few minutes later, the phone rang.

"I had a great time today, but I don't think we can meet up Tuesday night, unless you want to drive down here to Weston. By the time I finish work and drive in rush hour traffic from Fort Lauderdale to you in Delray Beach, our night will be cut short."

Just what I wanted to hear right now. Could this night get any better?

"I don't think I'm ready to come to your place just yet."

"So, are we good for Saturday night?" He asked.

"Sure, that would be great."

I felt a little discouraged. He seemed cautious. I wanted to see him again. Our chemistry was intense. The kissing was pretty amazing. But still— No expectations!

Mr. Five Love Languages called every couple of days. We flirted and chatted about our upcoming date.

After talking on the phone, I was getting a decent grasp of who he was. I had a good feeling about him, but I wasn't getting too excited yet.

"Can I come to your house and pick you up Saturday night?" He asked.

"I think I can let you do that. I've only let a couple of guys come to my house, so you should feel special. LOL."

"I appreciate it."

A day later—

Mr. Five Love Languages texted me—
Guess what I'm thinking about?

Me—
Do tell . . .

Him—
U want the G rated or the X rated?

Me—
G for now. Smiling.

Him—
I was thinking of your luscious lips and how I am looking forward to kissing u.

Me—
Really . . . hmm . . . I like that!

The anticipation was killing me. He was definitely pursuing me, and I liked it. His texts were playful.

However, I hadn't seen much of his personality yet. I needed to explore and see if he had a fun side.

The doorbell rang. The dogs went running and began their usual barking. I opened the door.

"Hi, come on in."

He had on very tight black jeans and a black paisley long sleeve button down with sleeves rolled up to his forearms, paired with dark gray suede boots. There is something sexy about a man in a great pair of shoes.

"Hi. Sorry I'm a couple minutes late. I changed my shirt a couple of times."

"Yeah, me too."

I had on a dark purple shiny top that accentuated my boobs, it tied in back, with a pair of black jeans; and high heeled, black pointy toed, knee-high boots.

He wrapped one arm around my back, pulled me in close, put his hand on my face, and began kissing me. *Hello to you too!* We were in full embrace. The dogs were still barking and jumping on him.

"I like the way you just greeted me. Do you always greet women like that?"

"Not always." He smiled, then bent down and petted the dogs.

"What are their names?"

"Cody is the white Bichon. He's a lover and very sweet. Pepper is the pretty black and white Lhasapoo. She's all of eight pounds and thinks she's the boss of Cody."

"Let's go to Atlantic Avenue. I want to go a place that's lively."

He opened the car door for me and then got in. He leaned in and began kissing me. That slow tongue action and his full lips were sucking me in once again. Still, an amazing kisser! He smelled so delicious.

"Okay, now we can go." There was a twinkle in his eyes.

"Are you sure?" I flirted back.

We parked and then started walking on the Ave. He pulled me in for a long make out session right on the street. He had game—way more than I anticipated. You can never predict with these reserved guys. He had a similar, calm disposition to Pretty Boy and Mr. Kosher Kondom.

I caressed the subtle dimple in his chin.

"Has anyone ever told you how sexy this is?"

"A couple of times, but I never noticed it before that." He blushed.

"You're kidding me, I'm dying to suck that right off of your face." I gave him a quick peck.

We held hands and walked all the way down over the Intracoastal bridge, into Deck 84, to the back of the restaurant.

"Let's sit at the bar and get a drink." He suggested.

"Okay."

"What would you like to drink?"

"A Lemon Drop Martini, thank you."

The bartender put the drinks down.

"I'm a lightweight, so I'll sip this slowly." I stated.

"You are? What happens when you drink?"

"I get happy. Cheers." I clinked glasses with him.

"Me too, I get really silly."

We both got a little buzz on, got a bit silly and flirted with each other. He gave me a few simple kisses every so often.

"I can see why you like to have a cocktail before dinner. You're much looser when you drink." I teased.

"Just wait." He gave me his "I'm-really-cute" look.

We sat next to each other at a table for dinner. We shared two different entrees. We talked briefly about our prior marriages. Our issues seemed very similar.

"I wondered why I felt so lonely in my marriage, so I started reading books and came across *The Five Love Languages*. Have you heard of this book?" He asked.

"No, what's it about?"

"I'll tell you the basics of the book. There are five ways of giving and receiving love. Words of affirmation–saying nice things to each other, compliments. Physical touch–affection, cuddling, massage, intimacy, and sex. Acts of service–running errands, housework, cooking dinner, etc. Gifts–giving flowers, a card, chocolate, simple things. Quality time–date night, weekends away, spending time away from distractions. What are the two most important to you?"

"At this point in my life, I'd say words of affirmation and physical touch. What are yours?"

"Same as you."

"Wow, that's a good thing, right?" I smiled.

"Oh yeah baby!" He leaned in and gave me a kiss.

"Well, so far it seems like we have a lot of things in common."

I leaned in and gave him several kisses back. I sucked on his lower lip, gently.

"I love those lips of yours. I can't get enough of them."

"Thanks."

Lucky for me, so far, no hang-ups!

"Let's share a dessert." He suggested.

"My favorite part of the meal."

"Let's go dancing. I love to dance." He stroked my hair.

"Me too. Let's do it."

We walked down the Ave holding hands and strolled into the outside area of the club.

We drank. We flirted. We laughed. We held hands. We danced. We kissed.

He had great rhythm. He was a great dancer. He was definitely seducing me, and it was working. Our chemistry and pheromones were surging. Before we knew it, it was after 1am. We left the club arm in arm and then drove to my house.

"It's kind of late for me to drive home since we were drinking. Do you mind if I stay?"

Dude, those drinks wore off hours ago.

"Well, I guess you can stay, since you've been seducing me all night."

"Me? We can keep it clean and just sleep together." He gave me his shy look.

Yeah . . . sure we can! I had no way to dignify his comment with any response. I knew his play. My willpower? Well, I had no willpower at that point.

"I'm going to shower." I looked at him.

I walked into my closet. I heard a door slam. The dogs left my side and went running. I snuck out of my bedroom and peered around the corner of the hallway to see the dogs at the front door. The door opened. There he was, sauntering back into my house, gym bag slung over his shoulder. I ran back into my bathroom so that he didn't see me. That was a very ballsy move! Wasn't he the presumptuous one! Never would I ever think this guy would pull a stunt like that! But he did.

He set the bag down. The dogs had their noses in the bag. He opened up his bag and took out his toothbrush. I put my head down so that he couldn't see me smirking. I had to control myself from laughing. Hysterical!

It was 5am. He fell asleep. I laid there wide awake; I couldn't sleep. I was too keyed up. I peeked at him while he slept. Luckily, peaceful, not a snorer. Finally, I shut my eyes for a short while.

He cooked me breakfast. We took a shower together. We washed and shampooed each other's hair. It was very sensual and sexy to touch each other's bodies. His six pack and well-proportioned lean smaller muscles turned me on, along with his round butt and strong legs. To pamper each other felt gratifying. I took out the blow dryer, grabbed a brush and started drying my hair.

"Here . . . give the dryer to me."

Huh? He gestured to give him the dryer and brush. He began blow drying my hair. I was astounded. When did a guy do this for me? Never!

"Now this is a real "act of service." You have a lot of very thick long hair." He smiled.

"Thank you. You have no idea how much I appreciate this right now."

I was so tired. I closed my eyes. I sat there in a relaxed state. I felt every stroke as he brushed my hair. I enjoyed every moment.

We headed back to bed for a nap. It never happened. Afterwards, we fell asleep. I woke up and looked around. He wasn't in bed. I walked out of the bedroom.

"I was hungry. I hope you don't mind."

He was eating a yogurt and watching TV in the family room.

"I guess you worked up an appetite." I smirked.

"It's almost 4, I'd better get going."

Yeah, my daughter is coming home soon."

We'd been together for almost 24 hours. I liked him. I was on a high.

He texted me—
I left my watch at your house.

Me—
I'll keep it safe. I had a great time this weekend.
Thanks for dinner, dancing and . . .

Him—
You are very welcome. I hope to do it again soon.

The next day the phone rang.
"Hi, Mr. Five Love Languages. How are you?"
"Fine. I think we jumped in too fast. I tend to have sex too quickly."
"Well, if that's how you feel we can slow it down. Can you clarify what you're getting at?"
"I guess I was being analytical. Even taking a shower together is something people don't do so soon."
"No kidding! Well, we can't take it back now. We can only move forward and be more cognizant."
"I agree. I had three breakups over the past few years, and they were hard to get over."
"I'm sorry to hear."

So, Mr. Five Love Languages, what you're saying is, you jumped in too soon and it crashed and burned? Maybe you didn't develop an emotional connection? That's what I was hearing. I got the sense he wasn't ready to be in a relationship—or at all. I wasn't so sure about him either. Besides, I didn't know if he was worthy yet anyway.

I met **The Badass Paranoid Guy** for lunch. Why did I entertain that date? Because I needed to keep my mind off of Mr. Five Love Languages.

The Bad Ass Paranoid Guy pulled up in his Harley as I was parking my car. He was dressed head to toe in black leather with hoop earrings in both ears.

We entered the restaurant and were seated.

"Can we switch seats? I need to sit facing the front door just in case. There was an incident one time. Now, I carry with me at all times." He looked at me with a fearful glare.

He's packing? That seemed extreme.

"What happened?" I asked.

"When my daughter was very young there was a shooting, and a girl was killed."

"Oh . . . did you have a personal connection to this girl?"

"No, she was the same age as my daughter."

As I listened, I knew this guy was not for me. I was mortified to think that this paranoid motherfucker could pull out his piece and shoot someone at any time. We clearly came from different places.

He walked me to my car. He kissed me goodbye. He was a good kisser. Of course, I kissed him back. Kissing is my specialty! Didn't I always kiss the guy even if I had no intentions of ever seeing him again?

A few days later—

Mr. Five Love Languages called.

"For the first time in my life, I have acquired a small amount of credit card debt, which I never had before. I've always been financially responsible. When I changed jobs a few years ago I took a pay cut. Since getting divorced, and splitting our incomes in half, now I pay child support and have spent a lot on dating and relationships. I wanted to let you know about my situation."

"Well, I hope you aren't telling me you have major money issues, because I just dumped The Marriage Coach after we went out for a pizza, and two of his credit cards were declined. I had to give him a twenty to pay the sixteen-dollar bill. We had a date the same night after you and I met for lunch. We'd been dating for six weeks."

Yeah, I let him know he isn't the only guy in town.

"No. I have a great job and career. I have no debt except one credit card. I want to pay it down. I'm just letting you know that I can't keep paying for very expensive dinners and drinks. I think it's only fair that if two people are in a relationship, it would be nice if the woman chipped in sometimes."

"What happened with all the other relationships? They never came out of pocket for anything?"

"Never. I realized they were the wrong personality types for me after doing some soul searching. They were all very selfish, argumentative, and expected a man to pay for everything. I hope you understand."

"I think I understand where you're coming from. I just wish I met you before all those selfish bitches. Now, I need to think about this. It does bother me that you're telling me this so soon, particularly because we're not in a relationship. We just met."

He was being straight-up with me. He was implying, this is who I am, take me or leave me. He didn't want to get hurt again. He was giving me an out, now before later. The red flag came out. I would have to deal with it.

Third date—

We went to a local bar and had a martini. I took a deep breath.

"I thought about our conversation concerning your credit card debt. I want to let you know, I'm an independent woman. I can support myself financially. I don't need to be with you, or any guy. I choose and want to go out with you, so I don't expect you to get into more debt because of me. I'm also fiscally responsible, so I get it."

"Thank you for telling me."

"If we were to go on vacation at some point, I'd be more than happy to pay for myself, but I wouldn't want to pay for you."

"I understand what you're saying."

He talked about his past relationship that had ended a couple of months ago.

"We were making plans to move in together. I was giving up my place and then she changed her mind. There were other things that surfaced over time. I realized she wasn't as giving as I thought."

"Why do you say that?"

"On Father's Day, she gave me dark chocolate as a gift and said, I bought dark chocolate for you because I like dark. She knew I only liked to eat milk chocolate."

"Wow, that's a good one."

"Yeah, it was all about her. She never drove to my house. I always had to go chasing to her on her schedule. There were other things also."

"Sorry to hear."

"I guess it wasn't meant to be."

"I guess not. It's better than moving in and it not working out."

"Yes, you have a good point."

We went back to my house. We were sitting on the floor petting the dogs. I leaned over and started to kiss him. The dogs began jumping on us and licking us. We laughed.

He got up. He bent down and took ahold of me. He picked me up, then threw me on the bed. He had a naughty smile plastered on his face. He hopped on the bed and cozied up next to me.

So much for moving too fast and having sex too soon. Our SLOW DOWN sex talk had little impact on our actions. We just couldn't say no to each other. Our sexual chemistry was off the charts. We spent another entire night together and explored each other more. Maybe we could develop an emotional connection? Time would tell.

The next day, I sent him a text—
I had a great time with you last night.

Him—
Who is this?

Seconds passed. Nothing! No response. More time passed. What the f? I was baffled.

Him—
Just kidding

Me—
LOL!

Him—
Yes, I laughed a lot for me, so thank you for putting a smile on my face, in more ways than one.

Me—
Any time, love ur smile.

Now that was a turn-on. He showed an amusing side to him.

A few days later—

I was cooking brisket a few days ahead of time for my annual Chanukah celebration for a group of 20 people, mostly friends. My phone rang.

"Are you sure you want me to come over on Sunday? That might be a bit stressful since we've only been dating a couple of weeks, and this is the first Chanukah without having your ex there?"

"Well, I think it's very considerate and thoughtful of you to worry about my feelings, but it's been a year. Besides, I figured since you don't have plans to celebrate Chanukah, I would invite you. I've never brought anyone home since I started dating. There will be a big group of people here. You will blend in. I think we should say we're friends and keep it light."

"Okay, I'm just making sure."

I knew it was a bit premature to invite a guy I hardly knew, but in those past two weeks we had spent two entire weekends together. My intuition was telling me he was a thoughtful, trustworthy, kind soul. I also felt like it would be a good way for him to see me in my element. I wanted to see how he handled himself with my group.

A couple of days later—

We were spending another weekend together before the Chanukah party on Sunday. My son was coming home Saturday night from college on his one-month break, and my daughter would come back Sunday morning from her dad.

We went for a drink after our sushi dinner. He held my hand and began talking.

"I know we are new. I'm curious, is there anything I can do better in the bedroom and is there something specific you want?"

"Well, as a matter of fact, I'm glad you asked. Everything has been great so far and there is always room to practice and improve, right?"

"Sure! I think you know me more by now. I'm curious about a lot of things, and always about sex."

"Yeah, I see that."

I told him my wants.

"That was pretty clear. I think I can accommodate. I think we were nervous with each other in the beginning."

"Yup. I agree."

How refreshing was it for a guy to ask what I wanted in the bedroom, instead of him sticking it in, cumming, and falling asleep? Real—fucking refreshing! Real—fucking satisfying!

"Now, you tell me what you'd like." I tilted my head to one side.

He got specific.

"I can definitely accommodate." I grinned.

We went back to my house. We spent that night and the next day exploring each other's bodies. We both got exactly what we asked for and then some! We moved together as if we'd been dating for much longer. It was like no other guy I'd been with before. We liked the same type of touching, kissing, and all that went along with it. It was a feeling I couldn't describe. We were having a lot of fun and enjoying each other. Different than the boy toys because I had feels for him already.

"Let's order dinner. I'll stay with you until you have to leave to pick up your son at midnight. I wouldn't want you to fall asleep."

"Thanks, that's very thoughtful of you. I'm exhausted from all of our fun this weekend. You outdid yourself."

"I aim to please."

"Thank you." I had a big smile on my face.

Finally, a guy who pursued me who was considerate and seemed to want the same things I did. He gave me a sense of calm when I was with him. He was a giver just like me. I was open and let my feminine side guide me. I let him be the man. I would enjoy it and embrace it for as long as it lasted.

December

Chanukah Celebration

I went to yoga with live music to start off my day. I wanted to balance my brain and had to get into entertaining mode. It would be a long day and I was tired before I even started.

The guests started to arrive. My dad, the potato-latke-maker-extraordinaire, and my son started prepping. My dad wanted to pass down his latke recipe and latke making tradition for Chanukah to my kids. My daughter was studying upstairs for finals. A couple of friends arrived. A couple minutes later, Mr. Five Love Languages rang the doorbell. I introduced him to my parents and friends.

I went back to the oven to check on the brisket. The beef smelled delicious and was permeating the kitchen. Out of the corner of my eye, I noticed Mr. Five Love

Languages standing quietly by the casual dining area. I felt his eyes on me intently—I flushed. He was crushing on me. It was a good feeling. Nervous excitement.

I was very busy getting all the food ready when my daughter came to see how the latkes were coming along. I introduced my kids to some of my friends. I motioned for Mr. Five Love Languages to come into the kitchen. I was a bit anxious but stayed cool on the outside.

"Kids, this is my friend Mr. Five Love Languages."

Mr. Five Love Languages was being cordial and attempted to start a conversation with them. My daughter started laughing.

"What's so funny?" I asked her.

She walked away mumbling under her breath. "Sure, some friend."

Embarrassing! Mr. Five Love Languages talked to my son briefly and then they parted. The rest of the night went well.

The following week, my kids were with me. Mr. Five Love Languages called.

"Hi, how are you doing." I greeted him.

"I'm doing fine. I had a good time at your party. Your friends are nice, and your parents are like mine. Your dad is funny about his latkes. I think your daughter was feeling uncomfortable about you introducing me as a friend. I think she knows better."

"Yeah, you know teenagers. They're smarter than we think. I've never brought anyone home to meet my kids before you."

A couple of days later, I snuck out to see Mr. Five Love Languages. We had a casual night. Again, amazing sex. I loved the way he smelled. He was always sweet and kind. I liked a lot about him.

"Text me when you get home." He said, as he kissed me goodbye.

I texted Mr. Five Love Languages—
I'm home.

Him—
That was too fast.

Me—
I took the car to 135 mph.

Him—
No way.

Me—
Yes way. 1st time.

Him—
I can't believe you did that. Did you really?

Me—
Yup!

I was exhilarated. Not only to drive my car fast, but to feel the excitement of a relationship brewing. I was on a high. I called him.

"Did I tell you I went to the BMW M driving experience in South Carolina? It was a lot of fun. There were only two women and 24 guys. I came in sixth place on the racetrack. It felt good to beat a bunch of guys."

"That does sound like fun. I love to race cars on the track."

December 24

I arrived at his house at 5:00 pm so we could spend some time together before his friend's Christmas party. We headed for his bedroom.

"It doesn't get any better than that." He smiled.

"Then I guess we won't be doing it ever again! That was a mind-blowing experience for me." I gave him a kiss.

The connection was like no other. There was an energy when we were together that was powerful. There was no way to describe the feeling. It was exhilarating and gratifying, and I'd never experienced it before. If you have felt it, then you would understand. If you have never experienced this feeling, then it's time to go and find somebody to feel it with.

We continued connecting on an emotional level. He told me about his career path. He had a master's degree in geology. Back in the eighties when the oil industry tanked, he changed careers and went into financial planning. Then, he ended up working in life insurance. He wasn't content with his current job. He wanted to get back in financial planning, which felt more rewarding, and he could make more money.

It was getting late; I had a 45-minute drive. He called as I was driving home.

"I have this dating book, so we can answer the questions to see what commonalities we have, and it'll keep you occupied on the way home."

Just as I parked in my garage, he said, "I want to take it slow. I just got out of this other relationship a couple of months ago and I don't want to get hurt again."

"I understand what you're saying. I'll just say this to you Mr. Five Love Languages. I'm living in the moment. I'm not thinking about the future. I'm enjoying our time together. That's it. Really. No worries."

WTF! Really? I was rattled, and confused, and upset. But he would never know it! I guessed that the mind-blowing sex made him really nervous, along with starting to connect on an emotional level. There was no other explanation. I knew he was into me—why else would he be spending so much time with me? Maybe the great sex? LOL!

I WASN'T GIVING UP SO EASILY! PERSEVERANCE!

I liked him a lot. I would give him the time and space he needed. I wouldn't rush him. I had to play it his way. Not really play him—it wasn't a game. I had to understand who he was to be with him. He was The Guarded Guy who was afraid of getting hurt again. What you see is what you get. This is me. Take me or leave me. That was the message he was conveying.

December 28

Mr. Five Love Languages and I had plans to have a low-key night together. I wanted to keep the mood playful and amusing. Predominantly after our serious conversations—and his serious reservations. I had the perception to tread lightly with this guy.

The temperatures had dropped into the 30's. It was rare for South Florida to see those temperatures. The phone rang.

"I might have to bring out my fur coat, it's so cold." I kidded Mr. Five Love Languages.

"It's not that cold. Aren't we staying in tonight?"

"Yeah, but I'm not used to these temps."

The doorbell rang. The dogs went running. I opened the door with an impish look on my face, standing in my stilettos. He stood there. He looked up—and all the way down. He had a big grin on his face.

"Nice look . . . I like your fur, but I don't think it's going to keep you very warm."

"Well, it's new. I've never worn it. I thought I would break it out just for you."

My smirk was so wide that the corners of my lips almost reached my ears. The brown bolero fur jacket barely covered my boobs—and my thong didn't cover much of anything else. He walked in. He pulled me in close and gave me a long kiss. He took my hand and led me into the bedroom. That was our low-key night.

There was something about this guy. It was the feeling I had when I was with him. He had a calming effect on my high-strung personality. He was always very responsive to me, which made me feel sexy and incredible. He was bringing out more of my sexuality. A continuation from The Gambler and Mr. Kosher Kondom. I started craving him, and the sex.

New Year's Eve

He carried that infamous gym bag over his shoulder. He immediately started kissing me and we ended up in bed. Afterwards, we cooked dinner and spent time relaxing before going to my friend's New Year's party.

After ringing in the New Year, we headed back to my home. Once again, we were in bed and finally went to sleep. He left for the weekend.

A week later—

There was a slight chill in the air. I put on a new clingy, sexy, casual dress, tights, and knee-high boots. Mr. Five Love Languages answered the door.

"You look great!" His eyes opened very wide.

"Thanks."

We hung out and once again found ourselves in bed. He started to have a serious chat with me about his money concerns. I listened while he vented. There wasn't anything more I could say. I heard it all before. It was getting old. It seemed like his fear of getting hurt again was still stuck in his head. Lucky for me—that orgasm put me in a peaceful state. I stayed unemotional.

"Let's go to Las Olas instead of the go-kart place. The way you're dressed up, we'll leave that for another time."

We were having a drink while waiting for dinner when he began talking.

"Maybe we should be exclusive, but date other people. I'm more than satisfied with you but my family and friends are telling me I shouldn't get into another relationship so fast."

"Well, I was dating other guys up until last week. I decided to stop. But it's no problem at all. I can get a date any day of the week. You do what's best for you and if that means dating other women, then go for it. If you find a better match let me know. I won't take it personally."

I kept as calm as I could and tried to stop fixating. The audacity! He wanted things just his way—to have sex with me and date others. It kept circling in my head nonstop. I tried my best to keep my feelings to myself so he wouldn't get alarmed. I played it very cool.

We went to a club down the street, had a drink, and danced for a while. The drink and dancing helped to soothe my brain, somewhat. It was 1am and I headed home.

Things weren't going my way. I was finally open and ready, but I had to remember that it took two people to have a relationship–not one. He was closed off. It was up to him to open his heart again. I knew I might get hurt; it was a big chance I was taking. It was time to leave my options open again.

I went out with **The Anti-Semitic**. After he said the word "Jew" 15 times on the second date, I was disgusted and finished with him.

Next, I went out with **The Maasai Warrior**. I thought we could connect because he climbed Kilimanjaro and I'd been to Kenya and Tanzania on safari. That didn't happen.

I continued dating and kept my assortment of men accessible, just in case it didn't work out with Mr. Five Love Languages. Maybe I would meet someone who was ready. Or, most likely, I would quit online dating and give it a break for a while.

January 17

I still felt down and didn't know how to feel about that exclusivity conversation. We definitely needed to hash it out.

I went to the grocery store. At the check-out, I ran into **The Hat Guy**. We had a lunch date a few months prior.

"You look really cute." He smirked at me.

"You look good yourself." I smiled back.

"Why don't we go out, get drunk, and have some fun together."

He was loading his groceries on the conveyer belt.

"Hmm. I'll think about it."

An hour or so later, he began texting me. I was very tempted. We had great chemistry. He was a great kisser. But, after our date, he ghosted me.

I was confused. I spoke to my therapist and told her what was going on with Mr. Five Love Languages and The Hat Guy.

"Forget The Hat Guy. The way he belittled you on that date . . . because you said he looked grayer in person than his pic after he was the one who asked you in the first place."

"Yeah, you have a good point. I guess I'm feeling vulnerable at the moment, which I haven't felt in a long time. Mr. Five Love Languages is wavering and is so afraid of getting hurt; I have no idea where we stand. I like him more than anyone I've ever met, but he just can't get out of his own way."

"I suggest you tell him how you feel."

"That's a scary proposition!"

"It might be scary, but that's the only way you'll know how he feels."

I was afraid of what I might hear, but I knew I needed closure either way.

January 18

Mr. Five Love Languages called.

"I'm on my way home from jury duty so come on down. I'm going to cook the fresh fish I caught while fishing with my sons on Sunday."

He opened the door and pulled me in. He started kissing me in his foyer. The kissing was great as usual.

I was trying to decide when I should start our discussion. I was nervous, but it was time to put the heat on. My stomach was churning. As we were eating the cookies I brought for dessert, I decided it was time. I took a deep breath.

"I really like you. We have a lot of fun together, a lot in common, we think alike, and it's easy with you. I'm curious to know about your feelings for me and where do you think we are headed? There's no pressure here."

"I'm not dating anyone else, and I'm content with the way we are. I think I should be dating other women, but I don't know why I'm not. You can still date other guys until you know if you want to be with me."

"I know I want to be with you, only you. I started dating again because you brought up that exclusivity crap with me. I haven't met anyone that comes close to what I have with you."

I paused. He needed a zinger! I waited another second or two.

"What would happen if I met a guy I like? Should I tell you I met someone who I want to have sex with?"

"No, you should wait a month or so before you have sex with him."

Ha, Ha, Ha! Is he a comedian? He should do stand-up!

"Oh really? So, I guess you want to have it all? LOL!" I kept the mood light.

Did he really have the balls to just say that? I think in his mind he knew that would not happen with another guy, or he was hoping it wouldn't happen. I stayed very composed.

"Well, as I said, I really like you. I want to spend more time with you. Every time we are together, we enjoy each other." I held his hand.

"You won't find a guy as good as me."

Finally! Something positive and profound comes out of his mouth.

"Probably not. I like you just the way you are. I like the confidence in that statement."

I put my hand on his face and gave him a kiss.

"I'm glad you like me for who I am. In the past, I got caught up and lost myself in relationships. I have some baggage from this last relationship, and I'm still scared of getting hurt again."

Yah think?

"I know you're scared, so am I. Rejection is scary, but I'm open and ready. If you ended this tonight, I would be hurt, but at least I know I tried because I've opened my heart. You should think about that."

"I like that you get me."

"More than you know. I would never want you to be anything other than yourself. I accept you for who you are. Don't change. We have our own lives; we won't suffocate each other. Play your tennis, do your thing. You don't have to come running to me all the time. You see how I drive to you and do things for you, don't you?"

"Yes."

"That's called compromise and commitment. So then, I'll stop dating other guys, yes?"

I put my hand on his face and stroked his face with my thumb.

"Yes." He gave me a peck.

Then, he gave me long hug, while stroking my hair.

I was feeling somewhat relieved. I was also proud of myself for putting my feelings out there, even if he crushed me.

We had a big break through—

January 19

Mr. Five Love Languages began texting nonstop. We texted back and forth all that day, which was more than we had done the entire seven weeks. He was sending me compliments one after the other. He was a new man. He was open, ready, and vulnerable.

I'd come a long way from one year ago and made huge strides over the past few months. Had I met him earlier that year, I don't think I would've had the patience or understanding for his guardedness. I might have blown it with him. I was so different with this guy. I really did get him! I had evolved to a place I'd never thought I was capable of.

There was always a calm aura emanating from Mr. Five Love Languages. It was a feeling of relaxation and well-being when we were together. It was an energy that I could not explain. I was very happy.

Almost two months had gone by. It felt like six months since we'd spent so much time together. Finally, we were more than just exclusive.

January 25

I met up with my friend Karen at J. Alexander's. We caught up on our week.

"OMG, we had marathon sex for three hours last Saturday." I giggled.

"What do you do in bed for three hours, can you explain?"

"A lot of kissing, affection, and love making. It flew by very quickly. It was pure bliss."

"Most people would never spend that amount of time in bed." She shook her head.

"Well, there are very special moments when you're looking into each other's eyes. It's eerie and unnerving at the same time, but we were connecting on a higher level. I know he's feeling me; it's scaring him senseless."

She had a puzzled look on her face. She still hadn't grasped the concept.

"It's the greatest feeling there is." I beamed.

January 29

We headed to the Ave for dinner. As we sat there, Mr. Five Love Languages brought up the future. He decided it was time to buy a house instead of throwing money away on rent. We would still live at least 45 minutes away from each other. It would be easier to stay close to the school district for his sons. I wanted to stay close to my daughter's school.

"You know I can't support you."

"I've told you several times that I don't need any man to support me financially. I can take care of myself. Besides, I don't know why you keep bringing up the future. It's way too soon to talk about this stuff. We've been together for two months. Buy your house. If you feel like you need to find a better paying job, then that's up to you.

Don't just talk about it; do something about it. We should be having fun and enjoying our time together now, not rehashing the same old."

"I guess so. I'm laying it all out here for you."

"I can see that. I've had a lot of things money can buy, but I got none of the things that money can't buy. I was miserable. I felt unloved and unwanted. I felt unvalued and unaccepted for who I am and being me. I know you like me and value me. I'm extremely confident about my body when we're together. I feel sexy and desired by you. You allow me to be myself and that's a great feeling. You are attentive and affectionate, and you fill me with all of the five love languages. You make me extremely happy."

"I hope so." He looked at me sheepishly.

"Well, if you don't believe we can get past this money issue, then maybe you should cut me loose. There's nothing more I can say." I said sternly.

There . . . I said it. Let me go before I get hurt.

Mr. Five Love Languages was stuck in his own head. The same thing happened to me too many times to count. I got stuck thinking of the WHAT-IFS, instead of the HOW-GREATS.

Overall, I still felt unsettled, but knew I'd been calm, collected, and said my piece; it was all I could do. It was up to Mr. Five Love Languages to figure out his life, and if he wanted to pursue me. Besides, it was up to me to decide if I would stick with him.

My decisions—
His decisions—

January 30

Mr. Five Love Languages left to go play tennis near his house and I went to yoga. I kept thinking about last night's conflict and couldn't stay in the moment during the class. I got ready and headed down to his house. I had a shitty feeling in my stomach, and I needed to confront him. Enough was enough! I did some deep breathing.

I walked into his house. *Stay calm.* I took his hand and sat him on the couch. I got on his lap, face to face. I put one hand on his face and the other around his neck.

"Can I ask you a question." I looked him straight in the eyes.

"Yes."

"Why do you keep bringing up the same old over and over? I don't understand why you keep pushing me away?"

I got choked up and began to cry. He held me. I put my head on his right shoulder. There were tears streaming down from my eyes onto his t-shirt. He lifted my head off his shoulder. He started wiping my eyes.

"Wow, I haven't made a woman cry in a long time. I'm sorry."

As he wiped my eyes again, I said, "we can't keep going around in circles. Either you're in, or you're out. Don't string me along. If you're going to break up with me, do it now. I'll be hurt because you've grown on me, and I like you a lot . . . a little too much, really."

"I'm going to try."

"I only want to be with you. Again, it's not about money for me. I would never want you to acquire more debt because of me. Do I like nice gifts, to be taken to nice restaurants, and travel? Yes. But there's more to life than just those things. For me, inner peace and happiness are crucial."

"You have a point."

"I can only handle so much of this talk and you being so guarded. I'll try my best not to hurt you. That's all I can promise at this point, especially if you keep up with the same rhetoric." I gave him another hug.

"I'll try to stop being afraid and open up." He held me again.

January 31

I had to cancel my plans with Mr. Five Love Languages the entire week. My daughter was sick, and it was my priority to spend time with her. Cody, our 12-year-old dog had to be put down suddenly. We all missed him, and Pepper had no one to boss around anymore. I missed Mr. Five Love Languages a lot, and I really missed his calming presence.

One week later—

"How about I cook dinner for you tonight now that my daughter is feeling better, and she went to her dad's?"

"That would be great. I'll be up to you around 7:30 depending on when I finish work. I'll text you when I'm close."

The doorbell rang. Pepper went running.

"Hi. I missed you. Dinner's almost ready." I gave him a kiss.

"Great."

He gave me one of his tight hugs.

"It's nice to feel you in my arms again. Long day and long drive."

After dinner, Mr. Five Love Languages was sitting on the floor petting Pepper. She was very needy. I sat down next to him.

"I'd like to take you to the mall and buy you jeans, a couple of shirts, and some sexy underwear. You'll keep them at my house if you stay overnight. It'll make your life easier. The clothes will be a pre-Valentine's Day gift."

My therapist suggested it would be a way of showing him I was committed.

"Wow, that's very nice. Thank you for your thoughtfulness."

"I know money is the big red flag in our relationship. I'd like to keep Valentine's Day to a twenty-dollar gift, a card and note to each other. Is that okay with you?" I suggested.

"I like that idea. Let me cook dinner for you. Can you come to my house and sleep over?"

"I have no place to leave Pepper."

"Bring her with you."

"Okay."

The next day, I met my friend Karen for our weekly dinner at J. Alexander's.

"Last night after we had sex, he teared up." I took a sip of water.

"That's a new one for me." She sipped her martini.

"Yeah, me too. He's finally opening up and showing me that he's in touch with his emotions."

February 12

I went to yoga to kick-start my day.

He texted—
I decided to skip tennis today. How about I come up earlier?

Me—
Sure. We can go to brunch.

We sat down with our salads and started eating.
"I'm going up to the buffet to get some hot food."
Mr. Five Love Languages left the table.
"Hi, how are you?"
Dr. Lucky plopped himself down in the chair next to me.
"When are we going out?" He asked me.
"I'm dating someone."
Dude . . . really? I knew he saw Mr. Five Love Languages get up and go to the buffet. I couldn't believe Dr. Lucky had the balls to sit down in Mr. Five Love Language's chair. I looked up at Mr. Five Love Languages filling his plate. Part of me was enjoying the moment, wondering what would happen when Mr. Five Love Languages came back and saw Dr. Lucky sitting in his place.
"I'm dating also. We should go out anyway. You should give me your number." He smirked at me.
He'd been flirting with me for months. His blond stringy hair looked greasy, and he seemed slimy. I looked up at the buffet. Mr. Five Love Languages was still adding to his plate. I didn't answer Dr. Lucky. I continued eating my salad. Dr. Lucky got up and left. Mr. Five Love Languages passed him on his way back.
The anticipation was killing me. Mr. Five Love Languages continued eating. He said nothing. I said nothing. I had no idea if he saw the whole episode go

down, or not. I looked around inconspicuously. I could see people whispering to each other.

I would occasionally run into Dr. Lucky on the Ave, sitting in-between two younger girls. I had no idea what he wanted with me other than another conquest.

February 13

The doorbell rang. The delivery man handed me a vase with a lot of very large red roses. Tears came to my eyes.

"Wow, these are beautiful. Thank you so much." I gave Mr. Five Love Languages a kiss.

"Did you know they were from me?" He gave me a tight hug.

"I thought so."

Later that day—

"Whoa, you look hot in that sexy white dress." He had a sparkle in his eyes.

"Well thank you very much for the compliment."

We went to dinner. He ordered champagne.

"We should go on vacation for our birthdays." He held both of my hands and smiled.

We were talking about the future, and it felt amazing. Our birthdays weren't for a few months. We both commented on the great weekend we were having. Just fun, no bullshit.

Once again at home, we were making love and enjoying each other.

"You're the most sensual woman I've ever met." He held me in his arms.

"That's very nice of you to say."

We were both keyed up afterwards, so we stayed up connecting and talking. Again, our relationship reached new heights. He was a bit giggly and silly like a man falling in love. He had finally let his guard down. Again, he thanked me for taking him shopping and for a great weekend.

I felt a positive shift—

My heart soared. I felt very happy. I wanted it to continue.

Valentine's Day

I packed to stay at his house overnight for the first time. I was excited. I was hoping Pepper would not freak-out in a new environment.

"I'm running late. Traffic's horrible. Can you believe my boss gave me last-minute work to do on Valentine's Day?" He sounded frustrated.

"No, but don't stress."

I got Pepper in her dog bed and drove to his home. When I arrived, Mr. Five Love Languages wasn't present. He didn't notice how nice I looked, which was not typical for him. He was wearing gym shorts and a t-shirt. He was looking in a drawer in his kitchen. Pepper jumped up on him. He petted her and calmed her down.

"I'm sorry, it's too late for me to cook. I'll order Chinese."

He seemed frazzled, which was unlike him.

"No worries, that's fine. We can eat whatever, as long as we're together; that's all that matters. Besides, we already did a lot of celebrating this weekend."

I wasn't expecting any more than he had given and done for me. He went way above and beyond our twenty-dollar limit.

He ordered food. He then opened a bottle of champagne. We settled in and relaxed. Mr. Five Love Languages handed me two cards, a small fabric bag with a heart shaped amethyst rock in it, along with this note.

Valerie,

I know we have known each other for about two months, but in this short period of time, you have shown me that you are an intelligent, beautiful, giving, witty, loving, fun and heartfelt woman.

I have been contemplating what to get you for Valentine's Day, and the gift I chose relates to you in so many levels.

It is attractive to look at, both near and far and from all angles. The closer you look at it, the more things you find to admire and appreciate about it. It radiates beauty from the inside out just like you!

It is heart-shaped, and you are such a loving person who gives so much love to your kids, family, and friends; the heart shape fits you well. It also represents that you have a piece of my heart as well.

It was created by the universe, and like you, it contains unique materials that make it special and one-of-a-kind. It took years to form and has gone through a metamorphosis to get to its current state, just like you have changed and grown to become the wonderful person you are today.

So, if you ever are feeling lonely or blue just pick up the rock and hold it in your hands and feel all the warm thoughts radiating from it. Place it next to your heart and let its' positive waves radiate through your body, knowing that love is flowing all around you and that you are very special or just look at it and smile when you think of some of our fun life experiences, we have shared with each other, and the many we will create together.

I just wanted to let you know how wonderful you are, and I appreciate you on many levels.

Love,
Mr. Five Love Languages

He opened his heart; I was blown away. There were no words. I began to freeze up. I didn't know what to do with the feelings. They scared me so. My stomach was tied in knots. I needed Pepto-Bismol.

I never felt this way about any guy. We had come to a great place in our relationship. We understood each other, had fun together, and liked each other for who we were. It was a great feeling and I had to embrace it, not be scared.

End of February

We were together for three months. It felt like much more since we had spent so many weekends together.

We went to a Bat Mitzvah. The photographer came to take pictures.

"Stand next to him this way and smile." The photographer said.

"Smile like you're in love." Mr. Five Love Languages looked at me.

"I do love you."

No response! *Awkward!* Was he searching for my feelings? I had no idea, but it was too late . . . I said it. That would be the last time I'd say that to him until it rolled off of his lips. My brain kept circling. That went on for an hour or so. I was having trouble shaking it off.

We danced so much that my feet were killing me.

"Now, this is love." He said, as he rubbed my foot.

I knew he could feel my nervous unsettled energy. I half-smiled back.

May

Things were going well. We were together for six months. We planned our first vacation for our birthdays. It was his idea to go to Zion and Bryce National Parks, to go hiking, ATVing, and canyoneering. I had gone repelling one time in Costa Rica down a waterfall. I was willing to give canyoneering a try and looking forward to quality alone time with him on our vacay.

The first day we did a challenging hike in Zion National Park. Canyoneering was our second adventure the next day. We met with our guide, a tall, thin, outdoorsy guy with red hair and scruffy red beard. He seemed very nice and excited to get us started. We geared up as he gave us instructions.

"Now, I'm holding the ropes, so you won't fall. Who wants to go first?" Our guide asked.

"I'll go first. I want to get the first repel over with. I have a fear of heights." I said to them.

I looked over the edge. I was nervous, but knew I had to go for it before I chickened out. I turned around, put one foot down, and then pushed off the edge of the canyon. I got to the bottom. I was shaking from my adrenaline rush.

Mr. Five Love Languages reached the ground. Wasn't so bad, right?"

"Nope." He gave me a hug.

We got to the next cavern.

"Are you ready for this one? It's a tall one." Mr. Five Love Languages asked.

"I doubt it, but here goes."

I didn't look; I was too scared. I turned around and jumped off with force. As I looked down, I realized I had a long way to go. I kept jumping from boulder to boulder. I got to the bottom and looked up.

"Holy crap! I did it." I said out loud to myself.

Mr. Five Love Languages stepped onto the ground.

"That was a 100-foot drop. Did you realize how well you did?"

"Of course, but if I'd known you were going to take me to such a challenging canyon, I would've said no. Somehow, you have a way of persuading me to do things I wouldn't normally do. Just like that scary hike yesterday."

"You feel gratified afterwards, yes?"

"Yes. I do feel a sense of accomplishment. Even though I teared up from my fear of falling."

"That's what it's all about." He smiled.

We continued hiking down the canyon. The rocks were far apart, and the drops were very long. Mr. Five Love Languages was very protective of me every step of the way, just like when we were hiking. We worked together to figure out the best way down without using ropes. He would take ahold of me and carry me off steep boulders.

We stopped to eat lunch.

"Are you married or dating?" Our guide asked.

"We've been dating about six months," I answered.

"It seems like a lot longer. I'm impressed that you get along so well for only six months. Tell me how it works for you."

"Well, we like each other for who we are. We think alike and have the same love languages. The most important thing is that she gets me." Mr. Five Love Languages told our guide.

"I do get him, and he gets me too. We aren't trying to change each other." I looked at them.

After returning to the lodge, we had a drink and snack, then love-making session.

"Whoa, that was even more amazing than usual. We are great together." I was smiling.

He was resting on his side, elbow on the bed, hand on his head, lying next to me with his other arm around me.

"It doesn't get any better than that. Do you know why?" He had a smile on his face.

"Yup, I do."

"Because we love each other. I love you." He said with tears in his eyes.

"I love you too."

I teared up and kissed him. We hugged each other for a long time. We were filled with emotion.

November

Our one-year anniversary

Mr. Five Love Languages wrote this note to me:

Valerie,

I do not know when I first started to fall in love with you. It did not happen at one instance, nor was it one specific thing that I can remember, it just happened, slowly growing, naturally from within my heart. The more time I spent with you, the more I wanted to be with you, and I did not like being without you. We always seem to have fun together and get along, everything was easy, no drama. Yes, your luxurious hair, beautiful eyes, and great body had a little to do with it. But your positive, generous, and thoughtful manner made me appreciate you on a deeper level. The fact that we can laugh together on a regular basis tells me how happy I am with you. What truly makes me feel special is that you understand me, except me for who I am, and let me be myself. To me that is true love and I love you deeply for that.

I am always proud to be seen with you and have you next to me. Your tenderness and sensuality are like no other woman I have met. I find myself daydreaming about our nights together and looking forward to your soft lips and wonderful kisses.

This past year with you has been amazing. Our trip to Utah and all the adventures we shared will always be great memories. Vegas was awesome, from the shows to the restaurants, it was very special. Your birthday gift of the race car driving will forever be one of my favorite lifetime moments. Valerie, I look forward to more adventures and creating more memories with you.

Happy one year anniversary.

All my love,
Mr. Five Love Languages

I'm an extremely lucky woman. To have met this wonderful guy at the right time, and persevered through it all, I feel grateful to have him in my life!

Red Flags
* Mr. Five Love Languages was guarded, and afraid of getting hurt again.
* Money.

Insights and Lessons Learned

❖ Mr. Five Love Languages was guarded, but my affirmations and kind words made him feel more connected to me and allowed him to bring his walls down. I had the gut feeling that he was the guy for me. I had the patience and perseverance to stick with him. I didn't push, nag, or rush the process. I let the progression transpire naturally.

❖ He spent within his means. I commended him for not wanting to get into more debt, so we adjusted our plans accordingly. I advised him to pay off his credit card, and he used his savings to do just that.

❖ Most importantly, we give each other all of the things that money can't buy. Love, affection, emotional intimacy (as opposed to unemotional transactional sex), kind words, acts of service, quality time together, and thoughtful gifts.

❖ We get each other! We accept each other for who we are and aren't trying to change one another. With a similar way of thinking and shared interests, it's the foundation of the fun we have together.

❖ Communication is key. I made it clear that I was into him, and what I wanted in the relationship. He did the same.

❖ By openly expressing my desire, and then love for him, it was reassuring, and bolstered his self-confidence.

❖ He made me feel sexy and desired. My sensuality and sexuality soared like never before.

❖ I set my boundaries. I was only willing to give him a certain amount of time to open his heart and let me in.

❖ We are both non-religious Jews, have similar backgrounds and lifestyles, which works well for us.

❖ In the end, there were no deal breakers.

10
EPILOGUE

As you have discovered in the pages of my memoir, my journey was unique in many ways, a one-of-a-kind. It is important to note that your own experiences will undoubtedly differ from mine, and while certain moments may have been disconcerting, I wouldn't wish those upon anyone. However, I also wouldn't trade or erase those experiences, because I have gained valuable insights and learned lessons that have shaped me into the person I am today. These experiences have been instrumental in my personal growth and development.

Over the past few years, Mr. Five Love Languages and I have fallen deeper in love. We have kept our connection going, and fill each other's "love buckets" constantly. It's been everything I've needed and wanted.

It took a lot of perseverance to maintain our relationship. Despite living 45 minutes apart for years, we made it work. We had to juggle our kids and their schedules. Both sets of kids have become adults, moved out of state, and are pursuing careers. There were lots of other interferences as well. Too many to list.

Then, when Mr. Five Love Languages took a promotion and was transferred to Naples on the west coast of Florida with a well-known financial services corporation, things became more challenging, primarily because he took the position without any real consideration for my thoughts or feelings. I was pissed. Downright fucking pissed. Really hurt. I was 59 years-old, had to drive two hours to be with him, and was alone during the week. It was far from ideal. We took turns driving to be with each other every weekend. It took me some time to get past the hurt feelings. Our connection was so strong, we were determined to stay together. A year later, he got a new job 10 minutes away from where I live.

Finally, life together became easier. Not as effortless as we would like. I still take care of my 96-year-old mom, and he is the caretaker for his parents, 91 and 86, both have different types of Alzheimer's. It's stressful. We work together as a team to support each other. There's no such thing as "perfect." It never will be.

We play Pickleball together. He's very patient, is a great coach, and has pushed me to be a good competitive player. We have made lots of single friends playing Pickleball who tell us (after seeing the love we share for each other on and off the court) that they wish they could find a love like ours. It's tough out there. Not much has changed about online dating in 13 years.

All of these years, we have created many memories together, and have traveled extensively to many wonderful places all over the world. We continue to enjoy being with each other. We both feel lucky to have found each other, and I can confidently say that these past 12 years have been the most peaceful, happiest, loving, and best years of my life.

Finally, I have to mention, even after all of these years, we still have great make out sessions and our love making is unparalleled! He's forever curious and always a giver. Like the very first time, Mr. Five Love Languages continues to walk into the house carrying that infamous gym bag slung over his shoulder, evoking a smile, and transcending me back to that unique moment. Every Valentine's Day and birthdays, we exchange cards and heartfelt notes, which brings tears to our eyes as emotions overwhelm us. Remarkably, he still blow-dries my hair now and then. A blow for a blow . . . quid pro quo! Just like he always said, "it doesn't get any better than that!"

EMAIL: VALERIEMARGO2023@GMAIL.COM

FACEBOOK: DID HE REALLY JUST DO THAT?

INSTAGRAM: @DIDHEREALLYJUSTDOTHAT2023

BOOK COVER DESIGNED BY: ADAMGMAN.COM

9 7 9 8 2 1 8 2 1 0 6 6 3